Implementing the K–8 Curriculum and Evaluation Standards

Readings from the *Arithmetic Teacher*

Edited by

Thomas E. Rowan
Montgomery County
  Public Schools
Rockville, Maryland

and

Lorna J. Morrow
North York Board of Education
North York, Ontario

National Council
of Teachers
of Mathematics

The special contents of this book are
Copyright © 1993 by
The National Council of Teachers of Mathematics, Inc.
1906 Association Drive, Reston, Virginia 22091-1593
All rights reserved

Library of Congress Cataloging-in-Publication Data:

Implementing the K–8 curriculum and evaluation standards : readings
   from the Arithmetic teacher / edited by Thomas E. Rowan and Lorna
   J. Morrow.
      p.   cm.
   Includes bibliographical references.
   ISBN 0-87353-351-8
   1. Mathematics—Study and teaching (Elementary)   I. Rowan,
Thomas E.   II. Morrow, Lorna J.   III. Arithmetic teacher.
QA11.I436   1993
372.7'043—dc20   92-30628
                                                       CIP

Printed in the United States of America

CONTENTS

PREFACE

In March of 1989 the National Council of Teachers of Mathematics published its *Curriculum and Evaluation Standards for School Mathematics.* The companion document, *Professional Standards for Teaching Mathematics,* was published in March of 1991. These documents were "designed to establish a broad framework to guide reform in school mathematics for the next decade" (from the preface of each document). We are now about one-third of the way through that decade. The NCTM recognizes that although the *Standards* documents establish goals toward which mathematics teachers can move, their message must be interpreted and expanded in documents that give direct support to classroom teachers.

During the 1989–90 and 1990–91 school years the *Arithmetic Teacher* carried a series of articles on implementing the K–8 curriculum standards. These articles addressed each of the K–8 curriculum standards by providing additional interpretations and offering suggestions for implementation. The articles were very well received by *Arithmetic Teacher* readers. This publication compiles those articles into a single document that can be used as a reference for ideas that may help bring the *Curriculum and Evaluation Standards* to life in classrooms. Each article is published as it appeared in the *Arithmetic Teacher,* with minor editing in a few instances. At the end of this publication is an annotated bibliography of additional articles that have been published in the *Arithmetic Teacher* and that include ideas for implementing the *Curriculum and Evaluation Standards.* We have organized the articles and the references in the Bibliography into groups of related readings rather than follow the chronological sequence in which they originally appeared. We believe that this arrangement will facilitate the use of the compilation and minimize the amount of repetition that might otherwise have been necessary in the Bibliography. We have used the following groupings:

1. "Themes That Cut across Mathematics" (problem solving, communication, reasoning, connections, assessment)
2. "Number" (number sense, operations, estimation, fractions, and decimals)
3. "Space and Dimension" (geometry, spatial sense, and measurement)
4. "Data Collection and Interpretation" (statistics and probability)
5. "Patterns, Relations, Functions, and Algebra"

In addition to the articles that have appeared in the *Arithmetic Teacher,* other publications have supported the implementation of the *Curriculum and Evaluation Standards.* Notable among those being produced by NCTM are the booklets appearing in the *Curriculum and Evaluation Standards for School Mathematics* Addenda Series. The following is a list of all K–8 booklets that will be available in the complete series:

- Seven grade-level books, kindergarten through sixth grade
- *Geometry and Spatial Sense*
- *Making Sense of Data*
- *Number Sense and Operations*
- *Patterns*
- *Dealing with Data and Chance*
- *Developing Number Sense in the Middle Grades*

- *Geometry in the Middle Grades*
- *Measurement in the Middle Grades*
- *Patterns and Functions*
- *Understanding Rational Numbers and Proportions*

We believe that as the *Curriculum and Evaluation Standards* comes to life in classrooms, the mathematics education of children will reach new levels of success. We wish to express our special thanks to the authors of the articles that make up this compilation. Their work makes this document possible.

1

Themes That Cut
across Mathematics

The Vision of Problem Solving in the *Standards*

Problem solving has been espoused as a goal in mathematics education since the late 1970s, with focused attention arising from NCTM's *An Agenda for Action* (1980). But problem solving should be more than a slogan offered for its appeal and widespread acceptance. It should be a cornerstone of mathematics curriculum and instruction, fostering the development of mathematical knowledge and a chance to apply and connect previously constructed mathematical understandings. This perception of problem solving is presented in the *Curriculum and Evaluation Standards for School Mathematics* (*Standards*) (NCTM 1989, 23, 75). See **table 1.** Indeed, as noted in the *Standards,* "students need to work on problems that may take hours, days, and even weeks to solve. Although some may be relatively simple exercises to be accomplished independently, others should involve small groups or an entire class working cooperatively" (NCTM 1989, 6).

A statement such as that quoted

Edited by **Thomas E. Rowan**
Montgomery County Public Schools
Rockville, MD 20850

Prepared by **Patricia F. Campbell**
  and **Honi J. Bamberger**
University of Maryland at College Park
College Park, MD 20742-1175

The Editorial Panel welcomes readers' responses to this article or to any aspect of the Standards *for consideration for publication as an article or as a letter in "Readers' Dialogue."*

TABLE 1
Problem-solving Standards for K–4 and 5–8

K–4 standard 1

In grades K–4, the study of mathematics should emphasize problem solving so that students can—
♦ use problem-solving approaches to investigate and understand mathematical content;
♦ formulate problems from everyday and mathematical situations;
♦ develop and apply strategies to solve a wide variety of problems;
♦ verify and interpret results with respect to the original problem;
♦ acquire confidence in using mathematics meaningfully.

5–8 standard 1

In grades 5–8, the mathematics curriculum should include numerous and varied experiences with problem solving as a method of inquiry and application so that students can—
♦ use problem-solving approaches to investigate and understand mathematical content;
♦ formulate problems from situations within and outside mathematics;
♦ develop and apply a variety of strategies to solve problems, with emphasis on multistep and nonroutine problems;
♦ verify and interpret results with respect to the original problem situation;
♦ generalize solutions and strategies to new problem situations;
♦ acquire confidence in using mathematics meaningfully.

above may conjure feelings of unease in many mathematics teachers. Given the already crowded curriculum in mathematics, how and when can a teacher include long-term problem-solving activities while still meeting all the other expectations of the school curriculum? The key is the approach taken to problem-solving instruction. Problem solving should not be an isolated strand or topic in the already crowded curriculum; indeed, as envisioned in the *Standards,* problem solving should pervade a mathematics program.

Mathematics as Problem Solving

Almost twelve years ago, Hatfield (1978) examined rationales for problem-solving instruction. More re-cently, Schroeder and Lester (1989) reexamined this pioneering work in light of the *Standards.* Both of these references define and distinguish among "(1) teaching *about* problem solving, (2) teaching *for* problem solving, and (3) teaching *via* problem solving" (Schroeder and Lester 1989, 32). It is useful to consider problem-solving instruction as characterized in these documents.

Teaching about problem solving refers to instruction that focuses on strategies for solving problems. For example, students may be taught first to consider the meaning of a problem and then to plan an approach to solve the problem. They are usually taught specific techniques, such as drawing a diagram, that they can use in their plan. In addition to actually solving problems, this instructional approach encourages students to think back on their solution process and to evaluate their actions as well as their solution.

Teaching for problem solving focuses on applications. This approach uses real-life problems as a setting in which students can apply and practice recently taught concepts and skills. When narrowly defined, this instructional model delays problem solving until after the introduction of a topic or computational skill and then presents a sample problem to illustrate the targeted method. Students are subsequently given similar problems to practice. The intent is for students not only to learn a host of algorithms but also to apply their understandings in a variety of contexts.

Teaching via problem solving also values applications, but not simply as a reasonable setting for using already defined mathematics. Rather, this approach uses a problem as a means of learning new mathematical ideas and for connecting new and already constructed mathematical notions. A problem can be used to initiate study of a mathematical topic, to examine one or more mathematical relationships, or to investigate mathematical ideas further. Students come to learn concepts, connect ideas, and develop skills as they solve carefully constructed problems that embody essential aspects of the mathematical content being studied.

What is problem solving as envisioned in the *Standards?* It is not simply instruction for problem solving or about problem solving. It is students actively involved in constructing mathematics through problem solving; it is cooperation and questioning as students acquire, relate, and apply new mathematical knowledge. Problem solving is a setting for communicating mathematical ideas, a context for investigating relationships, and a catalyst for connecting mathematical concepts and skills. For young pupils, problem solving should come out of everyday experience. As the students mature, problems should involve real-world settings and mathematical investigations. Problem solving is not a solitary activity, nor is it a singular strand in the mathematics curriculum.

Activities

Developmentally appropriate problems can create connections between the informal understandings that a child brings to school and the formal knowledge outlined by the mathematics curriculum (Fennema, Carpenter, and Peterson, in press). These connections create understanding in mathematics (Hiebert and Lefevre 1986).

Teachers of primary-grade pupils have numerous opportunities each day in which to generate interesting, real-life problem-solving experiences. Attendance patterns, style of shoe (tie, buckle, self-stick, or slip-on), temperature, and weather patterns are all everyday events that furnish situations for problem solving. Field trips are another source of problem-solving events.

Measurement and Seriation (Primary Level)

Some kindergarten and first-grade classes take field trips, such as a trip to a pumpkin patch in the fall. Such trips present an opportunity for comparing, measuring, predicting, and patterning, as well as for communicating mathematical ideas. Prior to a trip to the pumpkin patch, the pupils are told that they may select only one pumpkin each and that it must be one that they can carry back themselves.

How did you decide?

After returning to the classroom, the teacher asks the pupils to describe why they decided to pick their particular pumpkin. As the pupils respond, the teacher focuses their attention on the mathematics involved by reiterating and recording such words as *tallest, fattest, heaviest,* or *roundest.* The teacher also asks a pupil to point out aspects of his or her pumpkin to verify that it is indeed tall or fat or round.

How can we sort?

Once attributes of the pumpkins have been clarified through discussion, the pupils are asked to sort their pumpkins according to a given characteristic. Because pumpkins come in many sizes and shapes, the teacher guides the pupils to consider each other's perceptions, noting that the pumpkins can be sorted in more than one way. The key is to draw out the pupils' thinking, to encourage them to explain why a particular pumpkin may be assigned to a particular pile.

How can we order?

Seriation activities are done when the pupils order the pumpkins by approximate weight, height, or circumference. During this activity, the teacher's role is one of question poser and idea promoter. The pupils discuss approaches and decide together on the way in which to order the pumpkins, as well as on a way to record their data. The pumpkins are then reordered and recorded according to a different attribute. The teacher raises questions to facilitate consideration of the relationship between attributes and to encourage use of the recorded data. Is the tallest pumpkin the fattest pumpkin? If one pumpkin is fatter than another pumpkin, could it also be taller? Does it have to be taller? If one pumpkin is heavier than another pumpkin, does it have to be taller?

What do you think?

Pumpkin cleaning is another interesting mathematics activity involving measurement and cooperative grouping. This activity requires pumpkins of different sizes with their tops removed (one for each group of pupils), lots of newspapers, two or more spoons for each group, one pan balance for each group, wooden blocks, and one bowl for each group. First, the pupils are asked to predict which pumpkin will have the most "insides" to scrape out and why. They then discuss how they could find out if their prediction is close. This discussion leads to consideration of approaches for measuring the size of the pumpkins as a way of estimating and then as a way of measuring the quantity of their "insides." Measures of weight or capacity can be used for the insides. Each group of pupils scoops out the insides of their pumpkin, transports the "insides" to the bowl, and uses nonstandard units of capacity or weight, such as wooden cubes, for comparison. The scale is used for weight. The teacher then focuses the pupils' attention on devising a means of recording their data, both the size of the pumpkins and the capacity or weight of the "insides." Follow-up questions with the whole class should lead the pupils to evaluate their predictions and to relate the weight to the size of the pumpkin and to the measurement of the capacity of the pile of "insides."

Place Value (Intermediate Level)

Students' understanding of place value is a critical aspect of number sense that influences their ability to estimate and apply any of the four arithmetic operations. Although many useful manipulatives exist to introduce multidigit numbers to students, they are often used in an artificial setting that fosters the use of rules. Money, specifically pennies, dimes, and dollars, furnishes a concrete representation of place value that is meaningful to students, draws on their informal knowledge of base-ten relationships, and fosters exploration.

How many ways?

Teachers can use play money or actual currency in this activity. For either manipulative, a fixed amount of money is counted out to each small group of two to three students. The students are told how much money they are receiving in terms of the number of dimes and pennies. They verify that amount and are told that at the end of the activity they will be expected to count out that amount of money and return it to the teacher. Initially, this time also is used to verify that the students know the identity and value of pennies and dimes. Then ask the students to determine how many ways they could create $1.00 using only pennies, only dimes, or both. Some children may decide to make a chart; others may make piles of coins worth $1.00; others may real-

TABLE 2	
Number of dimes	Number of pennies
0	100
1	90
2	80
3	70
4	60
5	50
6	40
7	30
8	20
9	10
10	0

ize that they could make more piles if they had more coins and so may ask to use other manipulatives to simulate money. A frequent question during this activity is, "Do I have all the ways?" Avoid directly answering this question by posing another question, "How could you find out if you have all the ways?" Subsequent full-class discussion should focus on the methods that the students used. The teacher then records the combinations derived by the groups (see **table 2**). Follow-up questions include the following:

> What patterns do you see?
> What must be the sum of the values of the dimes and pennies in each row?
> What do all the penny amounts have in common? Why?

In this way students can draw out for themselves the ten-to-one relationship between pennies and dimes rather than listen to a rule.

What coins do I have?

This activity causes students to use and strengthen their knowledge of place-value relationships as they solve interesting problems. Students should have coins to manipulate as needed. The teacher should pose such problems as these to the class:

> "I have six coins. I have the same number of dimes as pennies. How much money do I have?"

> "I have six coins. Some are pennies and some are dimes. Altogether I have forty-two cents. Which coins do I have?"
> "I have seven coins. Three are pennies and the rest are dimes. How much money do I have?"
> "The bank contains pennies and dimes. I have eight coins taken from the bank. How much money could I have if I put two coins back in the bank?"

Students are expected to explain their answers and their reasoning in a full-class discussion, using either the coins or charts or verbal strings of logic. Continue sharing responses to underscore that many differing, yet acceptable, ways exist to solve these problems.

Spatial Reasoning and Logical Thinking (Intermediate Level)

This activity is not only a problem-solving activity but also an effective diagnostic task, as it reveals much about students' approaches to a problem and their persistence. It connects a variety of geometric and spatial concepts and encourages the use of experimentation, cooperation, and communication. It fosters persistence, deductive thinking, evaluation, and record keeping. Because this activity is open ended, it permits a great deal of differentiation, depending on the students' level of ability and interest, and fosters the development of mathematical vocabulary to simplify communication. Each child needs five 2-cm cubes or five 2-cm square tiles and sheets of 2-cm grid paper for the activity.

When are arrangements different?

In a full-class discussion the teacher initially identifies a single block or tile as a *monomino*. The students are asked what they think *mono-* means and then how many different ways a monomino can be arranged. This question leads to a discussion of what is "different," namely, whether the rotation of a shape yields a different

TABLE 3

Name	Number of blocks	Number of distinct arrangements	Shapes
Monomino	1	1	
Domino	2	1	
Tromino	3	2	

arrangement. Assuming that rotations do not produce distinct arrangements, students quickly see that only one way exists to produce a monomino. Next ask the students to use two blocks and find all the possible ways of arranging them so that one side of one block fits exactly against one side of the other block. Again the potential of a rotation yields much discussion regarding what it means to be a different arrangement. The teacher asks for a name for the two-block; *domino* is usually offered owing to its resemblance to domino game pieces. Finally, the task is extended to a three-block configuration, prompting the production of a table (see **table 3**) and the designation of the term *tromino*. Follow with an examination of other words that have the prefix *tri-* or *tr-* and their common characteristic.

Extend to four- and five-block configurations

Once the students are familiar with this line of probing, many are eager to predict that a four-block configuration is called a "quadomino." Students generally support their reasoning by refering to quadrilaterals. Although this term is not the one applied to the four-block configuration, this line of reasoning should be applauded by such comments as "That really makes a lot of sense. I think that is a perfectly good and reasonable name for a four-block arrangement. But, for some reason, it is called a *tetromino*. What do you suppose the prefix *tetra-* or *tetr-* means?" When challenged to find all possible four-block configurations, the students question each other as to whether arrangements are

distinct. The students should be permitted to explore, communicate, and cooperate prior to sharing their distinct arrangements.

The fifth and final set of configurations instinctively calls the grid paper into play as a means of recording arrangements. Further, students generally ask whether they have found all the arrangements, the twelve pentominoes. Rather than answer directly, praise the students for finding so many arrangements but ask them if they think they can find more. Encourage them to use their blocks to explore arrangements, to work together to compare results, and to tell why they think they have found all the distinct configurations. If some students finish the task while others are still working, give them an extension task using the grid paper. For example, ask them to cut out the shapes of the twelve pentominoes using the grid paper and find out how many different rectangles they can make from any three of the pentominoes. Once they feel they have located every three-piece rectangle, they can move on to rectangles made from four pentomino pieces. See "Pentominoes Revisited" by Barry Onslow in this issue.

References

Fennema, Elizabeth, Thomas P. Carpenter, and Penelope L. Peterson. "Learning Mathematics with Understanding." In *Advances in Research on Teaching,* vol. 1, edited by Jere Brophy. Greenwich, Conn.: JAI Press, in press.

Hatfield, Larry L. "Heuristical Emphases in the Instruction of Mathematical Problem Solving: Rationales and Research." In *Mathematical Problem Solving: Papers from a Research Workshop,* edited by Larry L. Hatfield and David A. Bradbard, pp. 21–42. Columbus, Ohio: ERIC/SMEAC, 1978.

Hiebert, James, and Patricia Lefevre. "Conceptual and Procedural Knowledge in Mathematics: An Introductory Analysis." In *Conceptual and Procedural Knowledge: The Case of Mathematics,* edited by James Hiebert, pp. 1–27. Hillsdale, N.J.: Lawrence Erlbaum Associates, 1986.

National Council of Teachers of Mathematics. *An Agenda for Action: Recommendations for School Mathematics of the 1980s.* Reston, Va.: The Council, 1980.

National Council of Teachers of Mathematics, Commission on Standards for School Mathematics. *Curriculum and Evaluation Standards for School Mathematics.* Reston, Va.: The Council, 1989.

Onslow, Barry. "Pentominoes Revisited." *Arithmetic Teacher* 37 (May 1990):5–9.

Schroeder, Thomas L., and Frank K. Lester, Jr. "Developing Understanding in Mathematics via Problem Solving." In *New Directions for Elementary School Mathematics,* 1989 Yearbook of the National Council of Teachers of Mathematics, edited by Paul R. Trafton and Albert P. Shulte, 31–42. Reston, Va.: The Council, 1989. ◗

Communication in Mathematics

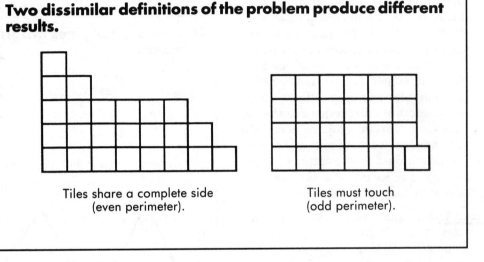

The dictionary's definition of communication includes such phrases as succeeding in conveying information, having social dealings with, making connections, and making known. Our mathematical definition of communication parallels the general definition. We want our students to convey their ideas about mathematics, deal with it in social contexts, make connections, and make known their thinking as they learn and become involved in mathematics.

The *Curriculum and Evaluation Standards for School Mathematics* (*Standards*) (NCTM 1989) identifies learning to communicate mathematically as an important goal. As we reflect on this goal and look at our efforts to furnish meaningful, student-centered experiences, we examine whether what we do each day in the classroom is taking us in the direction of better communication. We want to create an atmosphere where students are given numerous opportunities to communicate their own thinking and hear from their fellow students about alternative thoughts. This article discusses the importance of communicating mathematically and examines ways to develop this skill in the classroom.

Communication in and about mathematics serves many functions. It helps to (1) enhance understanding, (2) establish some shared understandings, (3) empower students as learners, (4) promote a comfortable learning environment, and (5) assist the teacher in gaining insight into the students' thinking so as to guide the direction of instruction.

1. *Communication helps students enhance their understanding of mathematics.* Expressing their ideas, engaging in discussions, and listening to others help students deepen their understanding of mathematics. Listening to the thinking of others opens up new avenues for consideration, which helps students appreciate that people think in different ways and that many situations have various valid approaches.

Students construct understanding on the basis of their experiences. Communication supports their construction of knowledge by helping them clarify their thinking. This process sometimes creates disequilibrium, requiring the student to come to grips with those aspects of his or her understanding that are unclear or partially formed. For example, after seeing U.S. census data on family size, a sixth-grade class decided to collect their own data from students in their class. Working in cooperative groups, they had to decide how they would display the class data. Many developed bar graphs. One group wanted to make a circle graph but struggled with how to make the pie segments represent the right amounts. They decided to write the percentage on each segment (because they had seen this done in magazines), so they wrote a percent sign after the whole numbers from their data. Realizing that their num-

Edited by **Thomas E. Rowan**
Montgomery County Public Schools
Rockville, MD 20850

Prepared by **Judith Mumme**
University of California—
Santa Barbara
Santa Barbara, CA 93106

Nancy Shepherd
Goleta Union School District
Goleta, CA 93117

The Editorial Panel welcomes readers' responses to this article or to any aspect of the Standards *for consideration for publication as an article or as a letter in "Readers' Dialogue."*

bers didn't add up to 100 percent, they wondered where they had gone wrong. Their dilemma prompted a rich discussion with the teacher of their ideas about the meaning of percentage. The teacher was pleased but knew that they would need many more experiences with percentage.

2. *Communication helps establish shared understandings of mathematics.* Many students fail to grasp mathematical ideas when they are presented as rules and procedures to be memorized and mastered rather than ideas to be discovered and shared. Our need to communicate with one another requires that we reach agreement on some aspects of mathematics (e.g., a numeration system, mathematical rules and conventions, definitions, etc.). By discussing and sharing ideas, students develop the need for a common language, appreciate the role of definitions, and eventually grasp the significance of discussing and clarifying assumptions.

Using square tiles, a seventh-grade class was investigating area and perimeter. Working in small groups, they were asked to find all the possible perimeters using twenty-four tiles. One group reported that they believed that only even perimeters were possible. Another group disputed this claim, indicating that they made shapes with odd perimeters. Each group explored these conflicting reports, using tiles to try to build shapes with odd or even perimeters. In a class discussion they discovered that they were defining the problem in different ways and that the results could be different, depending on how they viewed the task. Whereas some groups had decided that each tile must share a complete side with at least one other tile, as they had done with pentominoes, others had decided that any shape was permissible as long as the tiles touched (see **fig. 1**). By setting up open-ended situations, teachers help students grasp the significance of assumptions and definitions.

3. *Communication can empower students as learners.* When we ask students to talk or write about their thinking, we are telling them that we value what they have to say and communicate our confidence in their ability to think mathematically. By presenting what they think is important, students exercise greater power and control over their own learning, that is, they become empowered.

All communication in mathematics, however, does not necessarily promote empowerment. For example, in reciting the steps for doing the long-division algorithm, students can communicate that they have memorized these words but such recitation does not demonstrate their understanding of division or of when or how it is used. Contrast this exercise with students' explanations of how they could fairly share a box of raisins among five people or of the use of division to solve a problem in the real world.

Communication raises issues of control. For example, one teacher told his class that he had a friend who

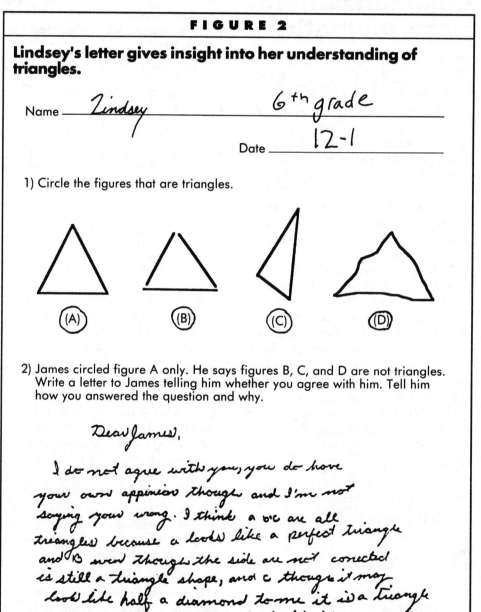

FIGURE 2

Lindsey's letter gives insight into her understanding of triangles.

Name _Lindsey_ 6th grade

Date _12-1_

1) Circle the figures that are triangles.

(A)   (B)   (C)   (D)

2) James circled figure A only. He says figures B, C, and D are not triangles. Write a letter to James telling him whether you agree with him. Tell him how you answered the question and why.

Dear James,

I do not agree with you, you do have your own opinion though and I'm not saying your wrong. I think a bc are all triangles because a looks like a perfect triangle and B even though the side are not connected is still a triangle shape, and c though it may look like half a diamond to me it is a triangle from a different angle. D looks like a piece of paper put in a blender but it can also look like a 1st grader drawing of a triangle so I think all of them look like triangles.

claimed that he had collected a million pennies, which he kept in his closet. The teacher asked the students whether they thought his friend was telling the truth. An animated discussion ensued about the size of the container necessary to hold a million pennies. The teacher wanted the students to discuss what they could do to decide whether his friend was telling the truth, but the students wanted actually to experiment with their ideas—to fill small boxes and check the space 100 pennies take up, measure stacks of pennies, even weigh pennies. If teachers want to encourage mathematical thinking, they should be willing to allow students to develop their own methods of investigation.

4. *Communication promotes a comfortable environment for learning.* Talking and listening to others in small collaborative groups is an anxiety-free way to try out new ideas—to test one's thinking. Interaction with peers is enjoyable for children. Comfort and security influence their willingness to take risks in sharing their thinking.

In the example in which a circle graph was constructed, the group structure afforded the students the security to discuss ideas with each other, to admit that they didn't quite understand, and to be comfortable enough to ask the teacher, "How do we make these numbers add up to 100? Please help us. We want to know."

5. *Communication assists the teacher in gaining insight into the students' thinking.* Teachers learn a great deal about their students by listening to them explain their reasoning processes. The ability to make these explanations is an acquired skill. As with most language facility, it grows with use and practice.

The *Standards* calls for mathematics instruction to develop students' mathematical power—the ability to "explore, conjecture, and reason logically, as well as the ability to use a variety of mathematical methods effectively to solve nonroutine problems. This notion is based on the rec-

ognition of mathematics as more than a collection of concepts and skills to be mastered; it includes methods of investigating and reasoning, means of communication, and notions of context" (NCTM 1989, 5). Communication—talking, writing, demonstrating, drawing, and so on—is the way teachers get a glimpse of students' thinking and determine how they are developing as mathematical thinkers. Looking at how students arrived at their conclusions helps teachers gain insight into the students' conceptions and misconceptions.

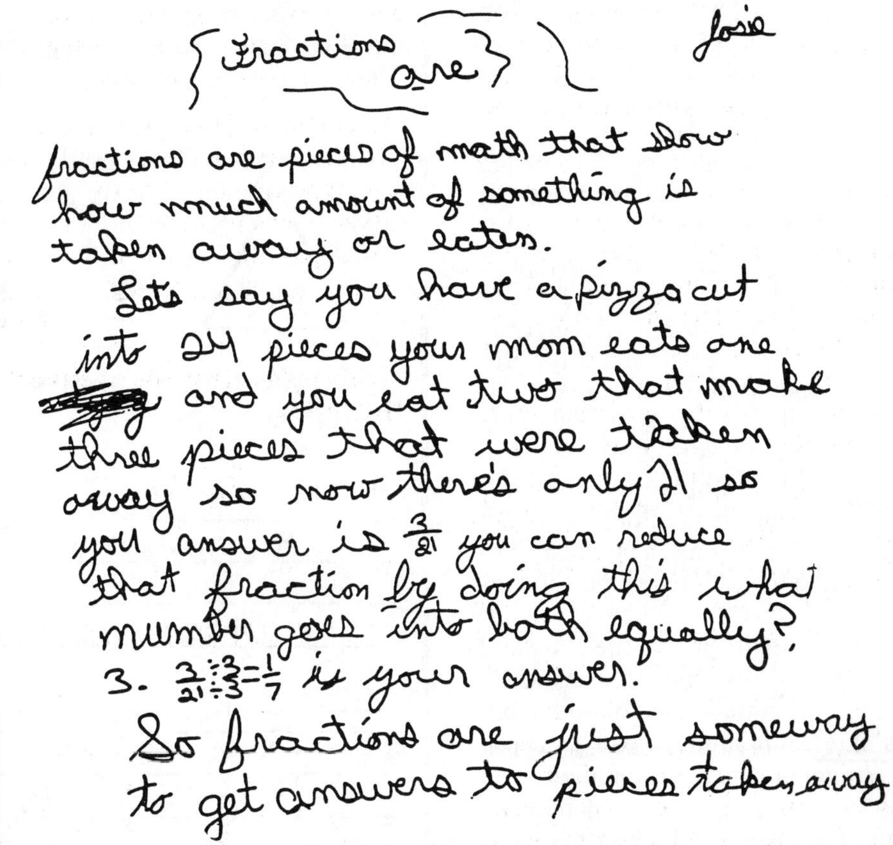

Figures 2–5 show some examples of students' writing that reveal some of their ideas about mathematics. In Lindsey's written response (**fig. 2**) we gain much more insight into her understanding of triangles. Josie reveals some misunderstandings she has about fractions (**fig. 3**). Even first graders can write about their mathematical ideas (**figs. 4** and **5**). See *A Question of Thinking* (California As-

sessment Program 1989) for further examples.

Fostering communication is an important aspect of mathematics instruction. Just as teachers plan the content of lessons, planning opportunities for students to engage in communication takes on increasing importance when we realize its significance in promoting learning. Communication can be fostered in several ways, including the following:

1. *Physical materials.* Using physical materials in mathematical tasks promotes communication among students by serving as a natural stimulus for talking. Students can be asked to describe a manipulative, tell what they discovered about its characteristics, what they did with it, and so on. The following is one way to use materials to encourage the development of mathematical language, spatial relationships, and communication skills. Two students pair up and place a bar-

---

FIGURE 3

Josie's description of fractions reveals some misunderstandings.

Fractions are
Josie

fractions are pieces of math that show how much amount of something is taken away or eaten.

Lets say you have a pizza cut into 24 pieces your mom eats one and you eat two that make three pieces that were taken away so now there's only 21 so you answer is $\frac{3}{24}$ you can reduce that fraction by doing this what number goes into both equally?

3. $\frac{3 \div 3}{21 \div 3} = \frac{1}{7}$ is your answer.

So fractions are just someway to get answers to pieces taken away

rier, such as a book, between them so neither can see the other's desk. One student builds a shape out of patterning blocks, or some other manipulative, and describes it to the other student while he or she attempts to duplicate it. Students take turns describing and duplicating shapes. Older students can be asked to write a description as though they were giving instructions over the telephone about how to make the shape.

2. *Interesting and relevant topics.* Investigations, project work, and tasks that are relevant to the interests of children are ideal vehicles for promoting student-directed communication. They help students to value mathematics as a subject that is useful in their lives. Information about the students themselves affords a wealth of possibilities for mathematical communication (e.g., hobbies, pets, favorite music, etc.). Many items that students use daily spark their natural curiosity. For example, a class activity that takes advantage of young pupils' interest in money involves pupils in designing and making their own play money in different denominations. They can use the play money to play store, count by multiples (to see how much money they have), invent or solve story problems, and so on.

3. *Questions.* Open-ended questions that allow students to construct their own responses and encourage divergent or creative thinking furnish fertile areas for communication. For example, questions like "What is the biggest number?" "What is the biggest number between 0 and 1?" or "What does *straight* mean?" permit many different ideas to emerge. Allowing students to pose questions leads to some interesting discoveries. Open-ended investigations can lead older students to some powerful mathematical thinking. Students start with a problem then extend it by posing their own questions to investigate. Two examples adapted from Pirie (1987) include (1) How many 1×1 tiles are needed to make a border around a rectangular pool? (Some students may choose to investigate rectangles of different sizes.) (2) Choose any number. Write down all its fac-

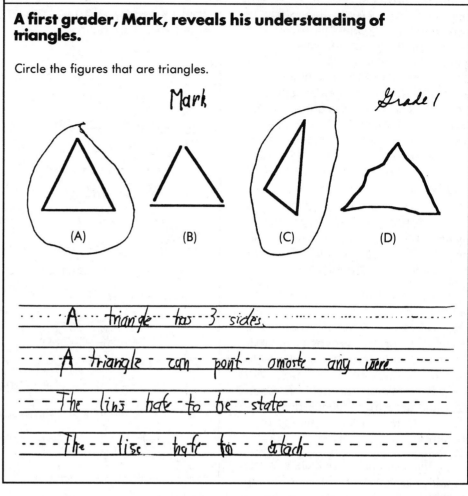

FIGURE 4

A first grader, Mark, reveals his understanding of triangles.

Circle the figures that are triangles.

Mark   Grade 1

(A)   (B)   (C)   (D)

A triangle has 3 sides.
A triangle can point amoste any were
The lins hafe to be state.
The lise hafe to attach

tors, including 1 but excluding the number itself. Add these factors to get a new number. Repeat the process with this new number. Investigate.

4. *Writing.* Written communication is important, and as students get used to writing, they grow to appreciate it as a part of doing mathematics. The teacher needs to help students understand why they are being asked to write—why explain it to the teacher, who already knows all that "stuff." Consequently, the purposes for writing must be made clear to students.

Initial attempts to write in mathematics can be difficult. A common response is "I don't know what to say" or "What'da ya mean?" To help students get started, make requests very specific. Asking them to write for an exact period of time, say, three to five minutes, is helpful. Have them complete a paragraph beginning with "I was trying to find . . ." or "This is what I did. . . ." Expand requests to

include their conclusions and feelings. Questions like "Why do you think your answer makes sense?" or "How does this material relate to our last unit?" and "How do you feel about . . .?" reveal much more of the students' thinking.

In *A Collection of Math Lessons* (Burns 1987, 1988), the author illustrates many examples of how she has students write about their thinking. Her books are excellent resources for teachers wishing to develop writing in mathematics.

5. *Cooperative and collaborative groups.* Classroom organization and groupings are important considerations in communication. Students seated in rows are not as likely to engage in discussions as students organized in a way that allows interaction. Small collaborative groups afford opportunities to explore ideas. Whole-class discussions can be used to compare and contrast ideas from groups

and for collaboration in such larger ventures as data gathering. Communication can also be aided by giving individuals time and space to explore, write, and read by themselves.

In the lower grades pupils work well in pairs. As they get older they can participate in various cooperative or collaborative efforts. *Cooperative Learning in Mathematics: A Handbook for Teachers* (Davidson 1989) has a wealth of information to help teachers.

6. *Listening.* John Holt (1970) once said, "Who needs the most practice talking in school? Who gets it? Exactly. The children need it, the teacher gets it." So, how does the teacher assure that the students are doing the communicating? One way is to ask them questions and listen. Encourage students to listen to one another. One technique used by some teachers is called a *dyad*. Students pair up, a topic is suggested, then they take turns listening and talking. The dyad can be timed, with one partner taking one, two, or more minutes then switching to give the other partner a turn. This technique can be used as a prewriting activity, to help students process their thoughts, or to help them address their feelings. For more information on the dyad, see Weissglass (in press).

7. *Overt and covert cues.* Teachers communicate their expectations and norms for the class both overtly and covertly every day in their classrooms. Our responses to students' questions, our classroom-management and discipline systems, as well as our methods of assessment, communicate important messages about what is valued and what is expected. These cues tell students whether communication is valued and whether they can communicate their ideas without anxiety.

No discussion of communication could be complete without addressing the issues of language and culture. As communication gains in importance in mathematics classrooms, many issues need to be addressed, among them, How do we—

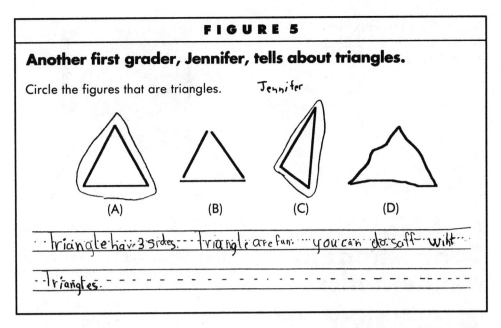

FIGURE 5

Another first grader, Jennifer, tells about triangles.

Circle the figures that are triangles.

(A)   (B)   (C)   (D)

triangle have 3 srdes. Triangle are fun. you can do saff witt Triangles.

- make sure that students are given sufficient opportunities to think and process their ideas using a language that allows them to construct meaning?

- assure that all students participate and have their opinions valued when working in cooperative groups in culturally and linguistically diverse classrooms?

- set up meaningful and culturally relevant learning activities that promote communication?

- meet the needs of non-English-speaking students and parents when the teacher speaks only English?

The following books explore some related issues: *Mathematical Enculturation* (Bishop 1988), *The Politics of Mathematics Education* (Mellin-Olsen 1989), *Designing Groupwork* (Cohen 1986), and *Linguistic and Cultural Influences on Learning Mathematics* (Cocking and Mestre 1988).

In the classrooms envisioned in the *Standards* students are talking, writing, and representing their ideas mathematically. The power to make this vision a reality rests with the teacher. Are communication skills valued enough to give them time to develop in the classroom? Is the teacher a model of someone who enjoys the thinking and communicating process? Does she or he value divergent thinking and see mathematics as a creative human endeavor? Teachers' success in developing communication skills in the classroom is based on their attitude toward these skills and the amount of class time they invest in encouraging and fostering them.

References

Bishop, Alan J. *Mathematical Enculturation.* Boston: Kluwer Academic Publishers, 1988.

Burns, Marilyn. *A Collection of Math Lessons from Grades 1 through 3.* New Rochelle, N.Y.: The Math Solution Publications, 1988.

———. *A Collection of Math Lessons from Grades 3 through 6.* New Rochelle, N.Y.: The Math Solution Publications, 1987.

California Assessment Program. *A Question of Thinking: A First Look at Students' Performance on Open-ended Questions in Mathematics.* Sacramento, Calif.: California State Department of Education, 1989.

Cocking, Rodney R., and Jose P. Mestre, eds. *Linguistic and Cultural Influences on Learning Mathematics.* Hillsdale, N.J.: Lawrence Erlbaum Associates, 1988.

Cohen, E. G. *Designing Groupwork: Strategies for the Heterogeneous Classroom.* New York: Teachers College Press, 1986.

Davidson, Neil, ed. *Cooperative Learning in Mathematics: A Handbook for Teachers.* Menlo Park, Calif.: Addison-Wesley Publishing Co., 1989.

Holt, John. *How Children Learn.* Harmondsworth, England: Pelican, 1970.

Mellin-Olsen, Steig. *The Politics of Mathematics Education.* Boston: Kluwer Academic Publishers, 1989.

National Council of Teachers of Mathematics, Commission on Standards for School Mathematics. *Curriculum and Evaluation Standards for School Mathematics.* Reston, Va.: The Council, 1989.

Pirie, Susan. *Mathematical Investigations in Your Classroom.* London: MacMillan Education, 1987.

Weissglass, Julian. "Constructivist Listening: A Non-Hierarchical Tool for Empowering Teachers and Facilitating Educational Change." *Educational Forum.* In press. ♥

Making Connections in Mathematics

At a recent meeting of a group of elementary mathematics leaders in Montana, one of them said, "I wish all elementary school teachers could realize how much mathematics they teach when they are not teaching the mathematics lesson. So many connections could be made between mathematics and the other subjects."

Startled by this statement, I asked what she meant by it. She went on to describe the connections between mathematics and three Mother Goose nursery rhymes, "One, Two, Buckle My Shoe," "I Love a Six-Pence," and "Going to St. Ives" (see, e.g., Wright [1916]). Each of these rhymes involves numbers and counting, and one introduces subtraction.

Students can write stories that go with simple number sentences, such as $6 + 4 = 10$. This exercise gives students an opportunity to write about mathematics and connect mathematical notation to their concept of mathematics as

Prepared by **Dan Dolan**
Montana Office of Public Instruction
Helena, MT 59620

Edited by **Thomas E. Rowan**
Montgomery County Public Schools
Rockville, MD 20850

Dan Dolan is the mathematics specialist in the Montana Office of Public Instruction in Helena, MT 59620. His primary interest is promoting the implementation of the content and spirit of the NCTM's curriculum standards.

The Editorial Panel welcomes readers' responses to this article or to any aspect of the Standards for consideration for publication as an article or as a letter in "Readers' Dialogue."

applied in the real world. Traditionally, most problems ask students to find *the* answer, and students are convinced that mathematics problems have just one answer. Giving students an answer, say, $0.15, and asking them to supply the question allows them to explain many different situations and problems.

In social studies, students deal with populations and with reading and interpreting various types of graphs. Reading maps involves measurement and

scaling; studying latitudinal and longitudinal lines reveals an application of angular measurement. Geologic time involves very large numbers. The combination of population and land areas lends an example of rate numbers in population per square kilometer.

Various geometric shapes can be combined in artistic drawings. The symmetry of figures can be investigated, and students can explore transformations as they flip, slide, or turn a shape to

---

FIGURE 1

Standard 4: Mathematical Connections

In grades K–4, the study of mathematics should include opportunities to make connections so that students can—

- link conceptual and procedural knowledge;
- relate various representations of concepts or procedures to one another;
- recognize relationships among different topics in mathematics;
- use mathematics in other curriculum areas;
- use mathematics in their daily lives.

Standard 4: Mathematical Connections

In grades 5–8, the mathematics curriculum should include the investigation of mathematical connections so that students can—

- see mathematics as an integrated whole;
- explore problems and describe results using graphical, numerical, physical, algebraic, and verbal mathematical models or representations;
- use a mathematical idea to further their understanding of other mathematical ideas;
- apply mathematical thinking and modeling to solve problems that arise in other disciplines, such as art, music, psychology, science, and business;
- value the role of mathematics in our culture and society.

FIGURE 2

Several representations of 4 × 2 = 8

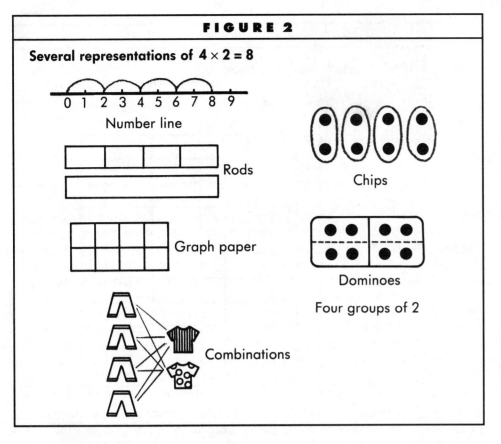

Number line

Rods

Graph paper

Combinations

Chips

Dominoes

Four groups of 2

match other congruent shapes. To prompt this kind of activity, teachers might wish to use NCTM's *Geometry in Our World* (Engelhardt 1987). Art also affords an excellent opportunity for constructing three-dimensional shapes and introducing volume and surface area. Music involves counting and patterns in rhythm. Songs, such as "The Twelve Days of Christmas," contain a variety of problems for students to discuss. In physical education, times and distances are measured, and such rate measures as meters per second are used regularly.

Science, economics, and business are full of applications of number concepts, computation, ratio, proportion, percentages, data analysis, probability, and the like. If teachers would use these many applications of mathematics in the world to remind students that mathematics pervades all subjects, they could reinforce the importance of mathematics and allow students to see connections within mathematics and between mathematics and other subjects.

A sixth-grade teacher in the group offered a specific example of a project she had used with her class that included mathematics, social studies, English, science, and library skills. The

mathematical topics included measurement, ratio, proportion, large numbers, and scale drawings. At her school one hallway between two buildings is approximately thirty meters long with a blank wall. She divided the class into groups of four and explained that a thirty-meter sheet of butcher paper would be cut into strips and given to each group; however, the strips would be taped end to end and strung the length of the hall. The project involved creating a time line that would display the time of the earth's existence and significant historical events.

Her students found that since the earth is approximately 4 billion years old, the number of years to be allotted per centimeter would be extremely large. After discussion the difficulties involved in representing 3 billion years to encompass the earliest life forms, or even 600 million years to encompass the existence of animal life on earth, the class decided to display a time line for the existence of humans on earth. The class first had to determine the number of years to be represented by one centimeter; then each group was given a portion of the time line to complete.

Science and social studies teachers

helped students to find significant events for their respective time periods; the library was used for research. People and events significant to the history of mathematics were included. Each group had to scale its particular sheet of paper so that the entire thirty meters used the same scale.

An eighth-grade teacher in the group described another project that involved science, social studies, mathematics, art history, forensic medicine, and the mathematical topics of measurement, fractions, decimals, ratio, and proportion. An article had appeared in the local newspaper describing the discovery of some human bones during the construction of a bridge. The local sheriff and an anthropologist from a university had been asked to investigate. Foul play was ruled out, and the few bones were sent to a forensic laboratory at the university. After much study, it was determined that a female had died 2000 years ago. She was approximately thirty years old and 140 centimeters tall and weighed 55 kilograms. Students were fascinated to know how such a determination could be made on such little evidence.

The teacher asked students to measure several body parts of each member of the class—height, length of the radius bone, length of the tibia bone, and so on. Several ratios were then determined, such as that of the length of the tibia bone to height, of the radius bone to height, of arm span to height, and the like. Although the numbers in fractional form were very difficult for students to analyze, conversion to decimal form immediately showed that the individual ratios were almost the same for all members of the class. The tibia was approximately one-fourth of the height; the radius was approximately one-sixth of the height; the ratio of the navel-to-floor measurement to height is one example of the golden ratio in the human body. It made no difference whether students were tall or short; the ratios remained the same (Neufeld 1989; Dolan and Williamson 1990, 74-78).

The work of Leonardo da Vinci, his study of the human anatomy, and the instances of the golden ratio within the human body (see Bergamini [1980, 94]) fascinated students and illustrated for

FIGURE 3

The area of triangle 1 is one-half the area of the shaded triangle and therefore one-fourth the area of the square.

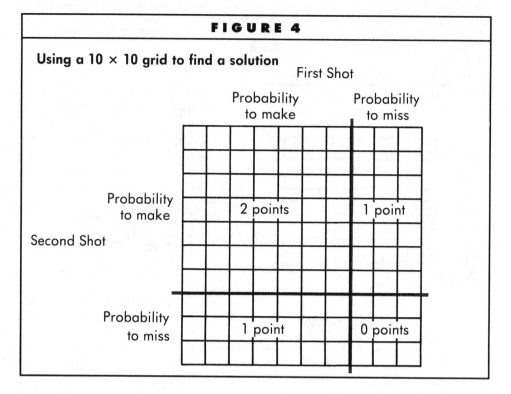

Triangle 1

FIGURE 4

Using a 10 × 10 grid to find a solution

First Shot

them the connections among mathematical topics and several subject areas.

Viewing *A Case for a Dinosaur Detective* (1986) from the videotape series Challenge of the Unknown extended this activity to the study of dinosaurs and the work of scientists in reconstructing skeletons and determining the speed of these large animals.

Pupils in grades K-1 often study themselves and the community in which they live as a part of a social studies unit. This investigation offers opportunities for many data-collection activities. The data can then be used to explore counting, graphing, addition, and subtraction. An example of such an activity is to explore the number of class members who come to school by bus, in a car, or on foot. The pupils can discuss their results in the context of their neighborhood and its geographic or other characteristics that help determine who rides in one or the other way and who walks. Even in some city schools where school buses may not be used, many pupils may ride public transportation of some sort, which can be substituted for the school bus in the study. As an art activity each pupil can make a three-inch-by-three-inch self-portrait that will be glued to a bar graph. The data can be counted, analyzed to

determine how many walkers live east of the school as opposed to west, and used in other similar activities. This pursuit, in turn, may also reveal something about the geography of the area. A variety of social studies or mathematics problems could be developed and studied, many of which can lead to addition, subtraction, geography, ideas about family characteristics, and so on.

Similar mathematical activities, such as planting seeds and studying their growth, can readily be found in science. The important thing is to recognize and make explicit the mathematical characteristics of the activities. If the mathematics is used but not made explicit, it loses much of its potential for enhancing and developing the mathematics goals of the curriculum.

These examples are clearly what is called for in standard 4 of the K-4 and 5-8 sections of the *Curriculum and Evaluation Standards for School Mathematics (Standards)* (NCTM 1989) (see **fig. 1**). The connection standards for grades K-4 (p. 32) and grades 5-8 (p. 84) call for the recognition of relationships among different topics in mathematics and the application of mathematical thinking in problems that arise in other disciplines. Too often students perceive mathematics as related only to the thirty-five- to forty-minute period of the day

involving computation or solution of word problems that have little or no relevance to their world (Frank 1988; Garofalo 1989).

The *Standards* also emphasizes that connections must be made among various topics so that students can see how mathematical ideas are related and how one mathematical idea can help them understand others (see, e.g., Bohan [1990]). Students in grades K-4 need several representations of a concept or problem to build understanding. For example, see **figure 2** for multiple representations of the same computational problem.

Geometry can be used to develop number concepts, fractions, decimals, percentages, operations with fractions and decimals, ratio, proportion, and probability. Tangram pieces can be used to illustrate equivalent fractions and introduce multiplication of fractions. Through careful dialogue, such as explaining how triangle 1 is one-fourth of the original square, students can model the connection between the idea that one-half of one-half is one-fourth and the equation $1/2 \times 1/2 = 1/4$ (see **fig. 3**).

In the middle grades, 10×10 grids are an ideal model to demonstrate percentages and the relationship between a percent and its equivalent decimal and fraction. Geometry can also present a simple solution to what may first be perceived as a complicated probability problem (Lappan et al. 1986).

The Spartans are behind by one point. Glenda, a 70 percent free-throw shooter, is fouled with no time left on the clock. She goes to the foul line to shoot two free throws. What is the probability that (*a*) Glenda's team wins by one point (she makes both shots); (*b*) they lose (she misses both shots), or (*c*) the game goes into overtime (she makes one shot)?

Statistics, fractions, decimals, ratio, proportion, percentages, and geometry are all applied in the solution of the problem. Data had been collected during the year to determine that Glenda was a 70 percent free-throw shooter; she had made forty-two free throws in sixty attempts. A chart illustrates the equivalent ratios:

Free throws made	42	7	70
Free throws attempted	60	10	100

The fraction 70/100 is equivalent to the decimal 0.70, which can be represented as 70 percent. The geometric solution to the problem again involves the use of the 10×10 grid (see **fig. 4**).

Summary

A focus of the curriculum standards is that mathematical topics should be integrated into various subject areas so that students can experience ideas from several perspectives and thus bring interrelated ideas to bear on new topics. This concept is reinforced in the National Research Council's *Reshaping School Mathematics: A Philosophy and Framework for Curriculum* (1990), which states that "moreover, instruction should be integrated so that relationships among different areas will be perceived and reinforced. For example, teachers should stress the use of arithmetic in geometry and probability, and the use of geometric concepts in the representation of data" (National Research Council 1990, 42).

References

Bergamini, David, and the Editors of Time-Life Books. *Mathematics*, rev. ed. Life Science Library series. Alexandria, Va.: Time-Life Books, 1980.

Bohan, Harry. "Mathematical Connections: Free Rides for Kids." *Arithmetic Teacher* 38 (November 1990):10-14.

A Case for a Dinosaur Detective. Challenge of the Unknown series. New York: W. W. Norton & Co., 1986. Videotape.

Dolan, Dan, and Jim Williamson. *Mathematics Activities for Elementary School Teachers.* Redwood City, Calif.: Benjamin-Cummings Publishing Co., 1990.

Engelhardt, John, ed. *Geometry in Our World.* Reston, Va.: National Council of Teachers of Mathematics, 1987.

Frank, Martha L. "Problem Solving and Mathematics Beliefs." *Arithmetic Teacher* 35 (January 1988):32-34.

Garofalo, Joe. "Beliefs and Their Influences on Mathematical Performance." *Mathematics Teacher* 82 (October 1989):502-5.

Lappan, Glenda, William Fitzgerald, Elizabeth Phillips, Janet Shroyer, and Mary J. Winter. *Middle Grades Mathematics Project: Probability.* Menlo Park, Calif.: Addison-Wesley Publishing Co., 1986.

National Council of Teachers of Mathematics, Commission on Standards for School Mathematics. *Curriculum and Evaluation Standards for School Mathematics.* Reston, Va.: The Council, 1989.

National Research Council. Mathematical Sciences Education Board. *Reshaping School Mathematics: A Philosophy and Framework for Curriculum.* Washington, D.C.: National Academy Press, 1990.

Neufeld, K. Allen. "Body Measurements." *Arithmetic Teacher* 37 (May 1989):12-15.

Wright, Blanche F., illus. *The Real Mother Goose.* Skokie, Ill.: Rand McNally & Co., 1916. ◆

Mathematics as Reasoning

Why is mathematics a regular part of standard elementary and middle school curricula? What do we believe, assume, or at least hope that students get out of the years of mathematics instruction that they are required to take? We often pose these basic questions to teachers at workshops, and after they get over their initial nervousness and uncertainty, most give one or both of the following responses: (1) mathematics is *useful* for people—as workers, as consumers, and as educated citizens; and (2) the study of mathematics helps people *develop the ability to reason,* and thus it helps them to become better problem solvers. These responses are not surprising, since both Dudley (1987) and Smith (1989) list them as two of the reasons traditionally given for the required study of mathematics.

The first justification, namely the usefulness of mathematics, seems obvious, at least for most of the mathematics that students study in elementary and middle school, although it can be argued that it is not always taught in the best ways for it to be most useful. The second justification, or more accurately the assumption, that the study of mathematics devel-

Edited by **Thomas E. Rowan**
*Montgomery County Public Schools
Rockville, MD 20850*

Prepared by **Joe Garofalo** *and*
David Kufakwami Mtetwa
*University of Virginia
Charlottesville, VA 22903*

The Editorial Panel welcomes readers' responses to this article or to any aspect of the Standards.

ops reasoning, is not so obvious. Although many people believe this proposition intuitively, it has been questioned by both Dudley and Smith, as well as many others, on the grounds that little or no scientific support can be cited for such a claim.

This article will not present differing viewpoints and arguments concerning this second justification. However, we believe that if we intend to help students learn to reason in mathematical situations, then teaching mathematics as rote memorization and reproduction is certainly inappropriate. Teaching mathematics as reasoning, as described in the National Council of Teachers of Mathematics's *Curriculum and Evaluation Standards for School Mathematics* (1989), is clearly more likely to take us toward this goal. We believe that it makes little sense to point students in one direction when we want them to move in another.

We have made a distinction between two approaches to the teaching of mathematics—rote versus reasoning. Similar distinctions have been made by many others. For example, Skemp (1987) distinguishes between two approaches that he believes actually teach two different kinds of mathematics, one based on instrumental understanding—"rules without reasons," and the other based on relational understanding—"knowing both what to do and why." He claims that instrumental understanding, which is the more popular, is easier to achieve, and because less knowledge is involved, it leads to right answers rather quickly. He contrasts these limited advantages with some of the more powerful advantages of relational understanding. Relational mathematics is more adaptable to new situations,

and once learned, it is easier to remember because when students know why formulas and procedures work, they are better able to assess their applicability to new situations and make alterations when necessary and possible. Also, when students can see how various concepts and procedures relate to each other, they can remember parts of a connected whole rather than separate items. Skemp also speculates that relational mathematics may be more satisfying intellectually than instrumental mathematics. Skemp's relational mathematics is consistent with mathematics as reasoning, as discussed in the following section.

Reasoning in the Classroom

To us, teaching mathematics as reasoning does not mean just including some reasons and underlying rationales when presenting mathematical material. It means involving students in activities that call on them to reason and communicate their reasoning rather than to reproduce memorized procedures and rules. Teaching mathematics as reasoning also means setting up a classroom atmosphere where reasoning is considered most important—that is, where it is valued more than getting correct answers. Such an atmosphere must be nonthreatening and supportive, and it must encourage the verbalization and justification of thoughts, actions, and conclusions.

The reasoning standard for grades K–4 (NCTM 1989, 29) states that the study of mathematics should emphasize reasoning so that students can—

♦ draw logical conclusions about mathematics;

♦ use models, known facts, properties, and

relationships to explain their thinking;

♦ justify their answers and solution processes;

♦ use patterns and relationships to analyze mathematical situations;

♦ believe that mathematics makes sense.

We believe that most students in schools will not develop the capabilities to perform the first four tasks unless they are challenged and guided to do so, a job that does not have to be as difficult as it may seem. Mundane tasks that can be solved in a rote fashion and tasks that do not require much reasoning can easily be modified or extended to require significant reasoning. For example, computational tasks, such as

$$\begin{array}{r} 23 \\ +\,18 \end{array} \quad \text{and} \quad \begin{array}{r} 235 \\ +\,183, \end{array}$$

can be made to entail more reasoning by the teacher's asking such questions as these: "Can you explain to us why it makes sense to carry the 1 in the first example?" "Is this also true for the 1 carried in the second example?" "Do these examples differ?" Properties of numbers can be used to elicit reasoning by asking such questions as the following: "Can you explain why $2 \times 3 = 3 \times 2$?" "Does this work for all pairs of numbers?" "Can you tell us why?" "Does a similar relationship hold true for three numbers?" Simple word problems can be augmented by the teacher's asking such questions as, "Can you explain to us why you decided to divide these numbers?" "Can you tell us why that operation makes sense?"

Another way to modify common tasks to involve more reasoning is to make them more open ended. For example, consider the following problem:

You are going to the store to buy a book, a pen, and some candy. How can you tell if you have enough money to buy them all?

Word problems like the foregoing cannot be solved by performing operations on numbers. Students have to reason about quantitative relationships.

For tasks such as these to be effective in helping students develop the kinds of reasoning we are concerned

with, teachers must be patient, flexible, and open to a variety of responses; however, they cannot accept responses that are based on rotely memorized rules or steps or on key words. Furthermore, teachers must be open to suggestions and challenges from students.

For grades 5–8, the reasoning standard (NCTM 1989, 81) states that reasoning shall permeate the mathematics curriculum so that students can—

♦ recognize and apply deductive and inductive reasoning;

♦ understand and apply reasoning processes, with special attention to spatial reasoning and reasoning with proportions and graphs;

♦ make and evaluate mathematical conjectures and arguments;

♦ validate their own thinking;

♦ appreciate the pervasive use and power of reasoning as a part of mathematics.

As we stated earlier, to develop the reasoning capabilities required for the first four tasks in the foregoing list, students should be actively involved in activities that call for such reasoning, and these activities can often be enhanced versions of more traditional tasks. For example, rather than just have students solve for x in equations like $x/9 = 4/x$, the teacher should also ask questions like the following: "Can you explain to us why cross multiplication can be used here?" "Can you explain why that procedure gives the correct answer?" "Can cross multiplication always be used with this type of problem?" "How would you solve the problem without cross multiplying?" Rather than just have students read values and identify points on graphs, teachers should also ask students to extrapolate from them to make and justify various predictions. Another way to use graphs to encourage reasoning is illustrated by this example adapted from Lowe (1988): "Invent a story to explain the shape of the graph below."

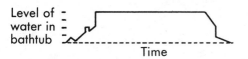

Teachers should also explain their own reasoning and give students opportunities to evaluate and comment

on it by asking questions such as these: "Do you think I did this correctly?" "Tell me how you would do it." "Why do you think that your way is better?" "Could both ways be correct?" Students can also be given written work to comment on in a similar way.

It is extremely important that such questions and activities not be limited to classwork. They should be prominent in homework assignments and in all forms of assessment. The makeup of tests, in particular, communicates to students which aspects of mathematics their teachers and school districts think are most important. If tests and other forms of assessment do not contain tasks that require reasoning, then many students will become convinced that reasoning is not very important. Also, without such assessment, teachers cannot effectively monitor the development of their students' reasoning capabilities.

We believe that the mathematics learned through such an approach to teaching has all the advantages Skemp attributes to relational mathematics. However, we also believe that such an approach can yield additional benefits. First, the act of explaining their reasoning gives students an opportunity to clarify and consolidate their thoughts and ideas and helps them uncover any gaps in their understanding and flaws in their reasoning. Second, teaching mathematics as reasoning fosters more appropriate and healthy beliefs about the subject. Too many students now hold unhealthy beliefs, such as that (1) mathematics is just memorizing and reproducing algorithms, (2) mathematics exercises and problems can be solved correctly in only one way, and (3) mathematical rules and algorithms are decreed by some authority. On the contrary, students exposed to mathematics as reasoning see that mathematics is sensible, and they see that they, too, can understand and invent it. They thus gain a feeling of power and control over their own future in mathematics. Third, in a classroom environment where explanation and justification are consistently called for, students are in a position to see the uses and value of such activities, and one hopes that the classroom experience will strongly influence their orientation toward their future mathematical learning. These last two benefits of teaching mathematics as reasoning are called for by the fifth points in both the foregoing lists.

Recently, on a television special that indicted the education profession for emphasizing rote learning and not teaching students to think, a student said to Barbara Walters, "I may be using my pencil, but I'm not using my brain at all." We believe that teaching mathematics as reasoning encourages students to use more than their pencils and helps them to become better mathematical reasoners.

References

Dudley, Underwood. Review of *Why Math?* by R. P. Driver. *American Mathematical Monthly* 36 (May 1987):479–83.

Lowe, Ian. *Mathematics at Work: Modelling Your World*. Canberra: Australian Academy of Sciences, 1988.

National Council of Teachers of Mathematics, Commission on Standards for School Mathematics. *Curriculum and Evaluation Standards for School Mathematics*. Reston, Va.: The Council, 1989.

Skemp, Richard R. *The Psychology of Learning Mathematics*. Hillsdale, N.J.: Lawrence Erlbaum Associates, 1987.

Smith, Michael K. "Why Is Pythagoras Following Me?" *Phi Delta Kappan* 70 (February 1989):446–54. ◗

Assessing Students' Learning to Inform Teaching: The Message in NCTM's Evaluation Standards

A central theme of NCTM's evaluation standards (National Council of Teachers of Mathematics, Commission on Standards for School Mathematics 1989) is that assessment is an integral part of teaching. One of the many reasons to assess students' learning is to find out where we teachers are in relation to our goals. Another reason is to be able to inform students, parents, or administrators about students' progress. Regardless of the relative merits of these and other reasons for assessing students' learning, the main purpose of assessment should be to inform teaching.

Educators commonly think of assessment as separate from teaching—as an activity that is typically done after a unit or chapter is completed or at specified times during the year to issue grades. But assessment that is most useful is continuous. Every lesson has built into it an assessment of students' progress toward the objectives of the lesson. Such assessment need not be formal. A teacher can assess students' understanding informally through their responses to oral questions or by listening to students' comments as they carry out a task. To

Edited by **Thomas E. Rowan**
Montgomery County Public Schools
Rockville, MD 20850

Prepared by **Alba G. Thompson**
Illinois State University
Normal, IL 61761

Diane J. Briars
Pittsburgh Public Schools
Pittsburgh, PA 15211

The Editorial Panel welcomes readers' responses to this article or to any aspect of the Standards.

obtain useful information, however, it is helpful for teachers to plan thoughtful questions and activities that have the potential to elicit the desired information.

Informal Assessment and Instructional Decision Making

A teacher makes many instructional decisions in teaching mathematics. Many of these decisions are made while the teacher plans lessons: What topic will be taught next and how should it be taught? What should the students learn, understand, and be able to do? With what subtleties of the topic are students likely to have difficulty, and how should those subtleties be treated? What questions should be asked? What tasks will be most helpful in enabling students to come to grips with the main ideas of the lesson?

Findings of research studies (e.g., Zahorick [1975]; Peterson, Marx, and Clark [1978]; Mintz [1979]) indicate that teachers seldom consider information obtained from assessment when planning or teaching. Yet if we expect to be consistently effective in our teaching, the instructional decisions we make must be informed and thoughtful. Ongoing assessment of students' learning is essential for obtaining necessary information to make wise instructional decisions. Informed decision making is based on knowledge and insights gained from both informal and formal assessments. Opportunities for informal assessment—

such as listening to students, observing them, and making sense of what they say and do—occur naturally in every lesson without teachers' having to plan and schedule time for them. Formal assessments, such as written assignments, quizzes, and tests, require thorough planning as well as a designated period to administer them.

Studies of classroom instruction have documented that teachers ask many questions during a typical mathematics lesson (e.g., Evertson, Emmer, and Brophy [1980]; Good [1981]). But for the most part, those questions require only simple rote responses that fail to give insights into students' understanding or lack of understanding of the material—they do not inform teaching. To discover the extent to which students are making sense of the material, questions requiring more elaborate, thoughtful responses must be asked. An example of one such question was asked by a fourth-grade teacher during a lesson on measurement. The teacher asked the students to explain the advantages of using standard units of measurement over nonstandard units. The ensuing discussion among the students was lively and informative. They remarked not only on the advantages of using standard units for purposes of communicating with others but also on the appropriateness or convenience of using nonstandard units. The students' comments revealed their understanding of many of the important ideas associated with the process of measuring (e.g., uniformity of the unit, iterative use of a unit, appropriateness of the unit size) and gave the teacher useful information about what the students had learned and what ideas needed further exploration. Thought-provoking questions must be designed and used deliberately throughout a lesson to assess students' grasp of the important ideas in the lesson.

Ongoing, informal assessment also calls for good listening skills on the part of the teacher and a tendency to probe and analyze students' ideas and responses. In a series of videotaped segments of primary-grade pupils working on mathematical tasks, Ginsburg and Kaplan (1988) show how information about pupils' understandings and misunderstandings can be gained through appropriate probing. In one case, a first grader presented with the numerical sentence $7 + 6 = 13$ is asked if this sentence is true, and he responds positively. The student then is asked the same question about the sentence $13 = 7 + 6$. He responds that it is not true, that in order for it to be true it must be changed to $13 + 7 = 6$! When shown the rearranged sentence, the student responds, "Now, it is true!" Through careful probing, it became apparent that the student's judgment of the truth of a numerical sentence was based on his notion that a numerical sentence must have two numbers joined by an operation sign to the left side of the equals sign and a single number (not necessarily the result of the operation) to the right of the equals sign. His notion of a proper sentence was bound to its surface structure, that is, to the relative position of the symbols. In his way of thinking, establishing the truth of such sentences had nothing to do with the numerical relationships stated.

Such a restricted notion may well be the result of the student's having encountered only sentences of the form $a + b = c$ and $a - b = c$, but the point relevant to this discussion is that such a discovery can alert a teacher to the importance of presenting a variety of sentences so as to prevent such misconceptions and of emphasizing the numerical relationships in each sentence. Thus, the information obtained can be used to make informed instructional decisions that are likely to enhance students' learning. It is precisely the informal assessment of the kind illustrated in this example that should be an integral part of teaching.

What to Assess? The Scope of Mathematics Assessment

In the process of assessing students' knowledge and how they think about mathematics, what should we look for? The curriculum standards offer help in deciding what to assess; they describe a broad range of cognitive and affective outcomes. But we must be careful not to reduce assessment to seeking information on specific and isolated skills, as in a checklist approach. Assessment, as envisioned in NCTM's *Standards,* takes account of students' mathematical knowledge holistically.

The message in the *Standards* is that knowing mathematics entails more than being skillful in performing mathematical procedures in isolation, devoid of a context. It entails more than being able to recognize examples of concepts and give definitions. It involves more than finding solutions to simple story problems. In short, mathematical knowledge entails more than the competencies that conventional assessments in mathematics have tended to emphasize.

The *Standards* states that mathematical knowledge includes *understanding* of concepts and procedures *plus* the ability to use these understandings to reason and think creatively and to formulate, solve, and reflect critically on problems in mathematics as well as in other disciplines. The student assessment standards indicate that assessment of students' mathematical knowledge "goes beyond measuring how much information they possess to include the extent of their ability and willingness to use, apply, and communicate that information" and the extent to which that information is integrated, that is, whether students understand relationships among various mathematical topics.

Classroom interactions among students and between students and teachers serve as natural opportunities for obtaining information relevant to assessing these aspects of mathematical knowledge. Those opportunities are not limited to the mathematics class. For example, one such opportunity arose in a sixth-grade social-studies class that was locating places on a globe using latitude and longitude. One of the students asked, "Are these *degrees* the same as the degrees we use with angles, or are they like the ones we use in temperature?" The teacher responded by asking the students what they thought. A rich conversation followed that revealed much

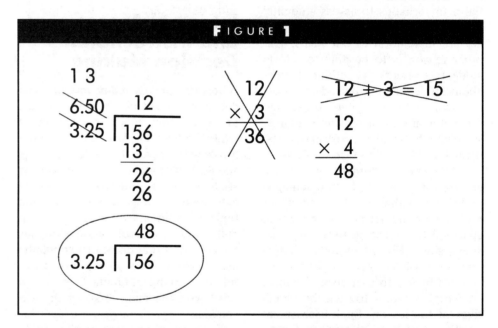

FIGURE 1

about the students' understanding of a variety of geometric and measurement concepts.

Assessing students' abilities to use mathematics to reason and think creatively requires flexibility on the part of the teacher. Students' creative responses and ideas are commonly judged wrong by a teacher because they do not conform with the answer or method the teacher expected. An example of such an occasion occurred in a seventh-grade class in which a student confronted with the task of dividing 3.25 into 156 carried out the task as shown in **figure 1**.

The student in question reasoned that by doubling the divisor he might eliminate the decimal. Since he did not, he doubled again, obtaining 13 as the new divisor. Feeling comfortable with a whole-number divisor, he proceded to divide and obtained a quotient of 12. At this point he debated how he should adjust his quotient to account for the transformation made to the divisor. After considering several alternatives, he reasoned that he should multiply the quotient by 4, thus obtaining 48 as the quotient of the original division task. Despite the correct answer, the teacher marked the student's work incorrect. As a justification the teacher offered that the student had failed to use the standard procedure that had been taught in class. One can't help wonder what effect, if any, this incident had on the student. It seems reasonable to assume that such incidents will discourage students from reasoning their way through a task in the future when memory of a specified procedure fails them. Recognizing and rewarding instances of creative mathematical thinking call for the teacher to be flexible and willing to probe, to listen carefully to sometimes-incoherent explanations, and to analyze those explanations.

Tasks for assessing students' mathematical knowledge (as described in the *Standards*) are not easy to design. The difficulty of designing appropriate assessment tasks, however, should not be used as a justification for maintaining the current emphases in conventional assessment practices. The evaluation standards offer examples that should be useful to teachers and others responsible for student assessment. The reform necessary to realize the vision of mathematics learning and teaching described in the *Standards* is unlikely to take place without undertaking a major revision of the aspects of mathematical knowledge emphasized in current formal and informal assessment practices.

How to Assess? Selecting Appropriate Methods of Assessment

Thus far, our discussion has focused on informal assessment. More formal assessments of mathematical knowledge must conform to principles to ensure that a reliable data base for forming judgments about students' knowledge is obtained. Our judgments are only as good as the information on which they are based. The general assessment standards present principles for selecting methods and designing tasks that yield quality information about students' mathematical knowledge.

One basic principle is that the assessment methods and tasks must be aligned, that is, they must be in agreement with the goals, objectives, content, and instructional approaches of the curriculum. Information obtained from tasks that are not adequately aligned with the objectives of instruction is of little practical value in informing instruction.

To achieve alignment, two aspects of the assessment need to be considered: the individual items and the instrument as a whole. Although the latter applies mainly to more formal assessments, such as teacher-made and standardized tests, alignment of individual items or tasks applies to informal assessments as well.

An instrument is aligned with a mathematics curriculum if it reflects the goals, objectives, and content of the curriculum and the relative emphasis given to various topics. Note that the instrument should be aligned with the curriculum, not the reverse. The curriculum must be determined before an assessment instrument is selected or designed.

Tests that do not adequately reflect the curriculum generate little information about students' learning or about the effectiveness of instruction. Consider the situation in which students who are using a curriculum that emphasizes problem solving, reasoning, communications, and connections among mathematical ideas as described in the *Standards* are assessed with a traditional standardized test. These tests typically place undue emphasis on tedious computational exercises under timed conditions and at best assess problem solving through performance on a relatively small number of story problems. Performance is judged relative to a nationally representative group of students (norm group). The students in question may score relatively poorly on such a test because they are not well practiced in doing tedious computation quickly or without a calculator. This test would also afford them little opportunity to demonstrate their problem-solving and reasoning capabilities. It is easy to see how this information could lead to incorrect judgments about students' learning and about the effectiveness of instruction.

Students who are classified as low achievers on the basis of standardized test scores often later "shine" in mathematics when they are fortunate enough to enter classes that emphasize problem solving, reasoning, and understanding over rote computation. Scoring poorly on a test that emphasizes computation under timed conditions does not mean that one is poor at mathematics.

Another fundamental criterion in determining alignment of an instrument is whether its individual tasks require the mathematical content that one is interested in assessing. Although judgments about alignment of content may seem obvious, they are not. For example, the item shown in **figure 2** does not adequately assess students' measurement skills. What do we know about students who answer this item correctly? Only that they can read a ruler. We know nothing about whether these students can select an appropriate measurement in-

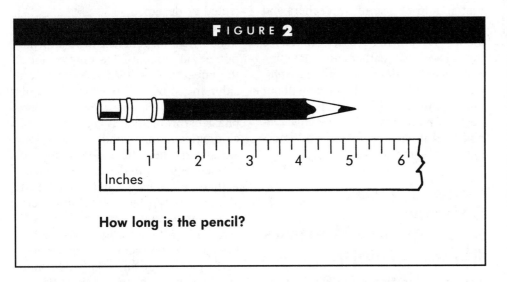

How long is the pencil?

strument, use it correctly (align it with the object to be measured and iterate it if necessary), and then read the result. We can be much more confident of our judgments about students' measuring skills if they are based on information obtained from a performance task that requires measuring. This example illustrates the importance of the method (e.g., paper and pencil, oral, activity) of assessment.

Many of the student outcomes described in the *Standards* are not amenable to assessment by paper-and-pencil tasks. For example, problem solving as described in the *Standards* includes formulating problems, using a variety of strategies to solve problems, verifying and interpreting results, and generalizing solutions. Therefore, judgments about students' problem-solving capabilities must be based on information about all these activities, not just on the correctness of their solutions. This information can be obtained from observing students as they work in various settings, including small-group, as well as individual, problem-solving sessions. Information should also be gathered from situations in which students are given a relatively long time, such as an entire class period or several periods, to work on problems and to extend their solutions. In addition, we should recognize that problem-solving capabilities develop gradually over time. To get information about students' growth, we should use techniques that are designed to show change over time, such as portfolio assessment. As its name implies, this method of assessment involves keeping a portfolio of students' work from different times and different settings.

Another factor that affects the usefulness of information is the possibility of students' responding correctly without using the mathematical knowledge we are trying to assess, that is, giving the right answers for the wrong reasons. For example, teachers often assess students' understanding of perimeter by asking them to find the perimeter of polygons like the one shown in **figure 3.** Their rationale is that students must really understand the concept to find the perimeter of a figure with so many sides. However, students often are more successful in determining the perimeter of many-sided polygons than of simple rectangles. Why? Because more than two numbers are given, and addition is the most obvious operation to use when dealing with more than two numbers. Thus, students can answer correctly with little knowledge of perimeter.

Some tasks in which students can respond correctly for wrong reasons are more difficult to identify. Consider this problem:

> Four of five dentists interviewed recommended Yukkey Gum. What percentage of the dentists interviewed did not recommend it?

A teacher asked one student who correctly answered 20 percent to explain her solution. She responded, "'Of' means multiply, so I multiplied four times five and got 20 percent!"

We infer the extent of students' knowledge from their responses to items on both teacher-constructed and standardized tests without information about the rationale for their answers. In such instances it is particularly important to examine tasks to determine whether it is possible for students to respond correctly without using the mathematical knowledge that we are trying to assess.

The usefulness of information obtained from assessments is also affected by whether the use of calculators and manipulatives in assessment is consistent with the cognitive objectives to be assessed and with the conditions of instruction. For example, consider a fifth-grade class in which calculators are always available for working on problem-solving activities, enabling students to attempt realistic problems with "messy" numbers without getting bogged down in tedious computations. The teacher also allows students to use calculators on problem-solving assessments because her purpose is to assess problem-solving capabilities, not computational skills. However, the use of calculators is prohibited when the goal is to assess students' mastery of computational procedures.

Rarely can a single task yield sufficient information for instructional decisions. Our confidence in our judgments of students' knowledge is increased when we find that students perform in consistent ways on a variety of tasks that require a range of mathematical thought, representations, or uses of a mathematical idea.

Tasks or sets of tasks must be sufficiently rich to uncover the extent or

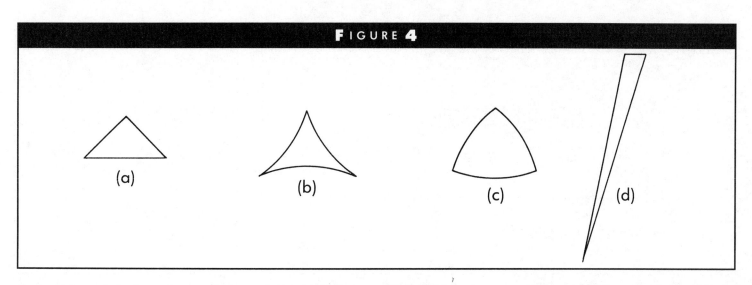

(a)   (b)   (c)   (d)

limits of students' understandings. Our previous example of the first grader judging the truth of number sentences underscores this point. If the teacher had merely stopped with the initial question (Is $7 + 6 = 13$ a true number sentence?) or had used only examples in the form $a + b = c$ or $a - b = c$, the pupil's faulty notion of number sentences would not have been discovered.

Consider another example, a pupil who correctly selects a triangle from a set of shapes including a square, a rectangle, and a circle. Apparently this pupil can identify a triangle. However, when presented with the item shown in **figure 4,** this same pupil responded that shapes b and c are triangles ("They have three sides") as well as a and that shape d is not ("It looks like a knife or a spear; it is too sharp to be a triangle"). Performance of the initial task alone would have led one to believe that the child had an understanding of the triangle; however, this single task was not sufficient to reveal the child's underlying misconceptions. This example further illustrates the importance of using multiple tasks.

A final consideration in the selection and design of assessment tasks is the developmental level and maturity of the students. Asking young pupils to "bubble" their responses on op-scan sheets imposes an irrelevant cognitive demand on them. Young pupils' understandings of mathematical ideas are often tied to the use of physical objects. Consequently, assessment tasks that involve such materials may

be better indicators of pupils' learning than other methods of assessment.

The results of assessment, either formal or informal, form the basis of our judgments about our students' mathematical understandings. Discrepancies in performance on different tasks can supply information on which to base instructional decisions. Consider a student who correctly finds the area of rectangles and squares yet cannot find the area of irregular figures drawn on a grid or build figures of specified areas with tiles. These results suggest that the student may not have a clear idea of area, although he may know relevant area formulas. This judgment is the basis for giving this student instructional activities that emphasize the idea of area as covering. If most students in the class have similar performance patterns on these items, an appropriate decision would be to devote class time to the development of the concept of area.

Conclusion

The evaluation standards present a vision of the kind of assessment that is essential for the implementation of NCTM's *Standards*. Central themes are that assessment should be an integral part of instruction and that its main purpose is to obtain data for making informed instructional decisions.

As illustrated in the foregoing, we as teachers can begin to implement the evaluation standards right now in our classrooms. We do not need to

wait for new instructional materials to be developed or special materials to be purchased. Rather we need to recognize the importance of continuous informal assessment, be aware of assessment opportunities during instruction, thoughtfully plan the selection and design of assessment tasks, be sensitive to students' responses and to the opportunities to probe further to gather additional information about students' mathematical knowledge, and be willing to use the information gathered in making instructional decisions.

References

Evertson, Carolyn M., Edmund T. Emmer, and Jere E. Brophy. "Predictors of Effective Teaching in Junior High Mathematics Classrooms." *Journal for Research in Mathematics Education* 11 (May 1980):167–78.

Ginsburg, Herbert, and Rochelle Kaplan, producers. *Children's Mathematical Thinking: Video Workshops for Educators.* Videotape. New York: Teacher's College, Columbia University, 1988.

Good, Thomas L. "Teacher Expectations and Student Perceptions: A Decade of Research." *Educational Leadership* 38 (February 1981): 415–22.

Mintz, Susan Levy. "Teacher Planning: A Simulation Study." Paper presented at the annual meeting of the American Educational Research Association, San Francisco, April 1979. ERIC no. ED 170 276.

National Council of Teachers of Mathematics, Commission on Standards for School Mathematics. *Curriculum and Evaluation Standards for School Mathematics.* Reston, Va.: The Council, 1989.

Peterson, Penelope L., R. W. Marx, and Christopher M. Clark. "Teacher Planning, Teacher Behavior, and Student Achievement." *American Educational Research Journal* 15 (Summer 1978):417–32.

Zahorik, John A. "Teachers' Planning Models." *Educational Leadership* 33 (November 1975):134–39. ▰

Number

Number Representations and Relationships

Using numbers meaningfully and flexibly is addressed in three of the NCTM's curriculum standards for K–4 and 5–8 mathematics (NCTM 1989, 38, 87, 91). The intent in this article is to give activities that are in the spirit of the *Curriculum and Evaluation Standards* and involve number relationships and representations of numbers.

Two recent studies indicate the positive effects of instruction that focuses on part-whole number relationships. One study of kindergarten pupils examined the effects that activities to develop part-whole number relationships have on understanding number concepts and addition and subtraction (Fischer 1990). The activities involved exploring partitions of numbers. For example, as these pupils were learning about the number 5, they separated sets of five objects into such parts as four and one, two and three, three and two, and so on. Students with these part-whole experiences had significantly higher achievement on assessment items involving number concepts, addition and subtraction word problems, and place-value concepts than did pupils without these experiences.

Prepared by **Edward C. Rathmell** *and* **Larry P. Leutzinger**
University of Northern Iowa
Cedar Falls, IA 50614

Edited by **Thomas E. Rowan**
Montgomery County Public Schools
Rockville, MD 20850

The Editorial Panel welcomes readers' responses to this article or to any aspect of the Curriculum and Evaluation Standards for consideration for publication as an article or as a letter in "Readers' Dialogue."

A study at the fourth-grade level found that students who studied part-whole relationships performed significantly better on tests of one- and two-step word problems than did students without such part-whole experiences (Huinker 1990). Studying part-whole number relationships can also foster a better understanding of fractions, decimals, ratios, and percentages.

A teaching experiment by Mathison (1987) helped middle school students learn to use and relate different representations of fractions, decimals, and percentages. These students developed an understanding of percentages by building on their prior knowledge and by using region models for fractions and decimals. The connections they developed among these models enabled them to make sense of a variety of symbolic and problem situations. Activities emphasizing meaningful connections among different representations of numbers can also foster a better understanding of whole numbers.

The following activities on number relationships and representations incorporate the first four curriculum standards: solving problems, reasoning, communicating, and making connections. Incorporating these standards increases the opportunity for meaningful learning and decreases the chance that students will depend on rote memory and learn isolated skills.

K–4 Activities

1. Give each pair of students six red and six blue connecting cubes. Have the students make a train that has exactly six cubes, keeping all the red cubes together and all the blue cubes together

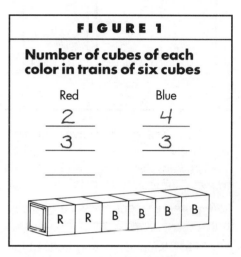

in the train. (Variations of these activities are possible without this restriction.) The students then record in the chart in **figure 1** the number of red and blue cubes in their train.

Problem solving. Ask students questions like these, discussing their responses as a class:

• How many different trains of six cubes are possible? Show them all in the chart. How many different trains of seven cubes can be made with the cubes you were given? How does that number compare with the number of trains of six cubes?

• If you cover the middle four cubes of a six-cube train, how many of the covered cubes are red? Blue? What are the possibilities? Can you determine which possibility is correct?

Communication. Lead students in this activity.

• Draw pictures of the trains you made. Explain how you knew when you had drawn all possible trains of six cubes.

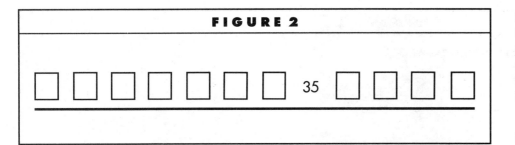

FIGURE 2

35

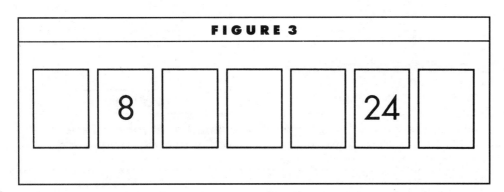

FIGURE 3

8   24

• Describe a train and have your partner draw it.

• Tell your partner in how many ways trains of eight cubes can be made.

Reasoning. Continue asking questions.

• What happens if you add a blue cube to a six-cube train?

• If you add a blue cube, what must you do to keep the train six cubes long?

• Turn one of the trains around. How is it different? How is it the same?

• Which six-cube train has exactly two more blue cubes than red cubes? Which six-cube train has exactly one more red cube than blue cubes?

Connections. Give students the following instructions and ask questions like these:

• Pick one train of six cubes. Cover all cubes of one color. How many cubes are covered? How do you know?

• Write an addition sentence to match each train. Write a subtraction sentence for one train.

• Pretend that the trains are birds. Write a story about the numbers of birds.

2. Using a card for each multiple of 5, construct a number line of as many cards as you wish. Place the cards facedown in order (see **fig. 2**). Tell the students that this number line shows

counting by fives. Turn over one card. Point to another card. Ask, What number is on this card? Turn the card faceup as the student answers. Repeat until all cards are faceup. Discuss the pattern of numbers.

Problem solving. Ask students questions about the number line.

• What number would be on the fourth card past 35? On the tenth card past 35? Will the number on the twenty-fifth card past 35 be odd or even?

• (Turn over two cards.) What is one counting number between these two numbers that is closer to the larger?

• (Turn all the cards faceup.) How many counting numbers would be needed to fill in the gaps?

Communication. Construct a number line of cards with multiples of 2. Place the cards facedown in order. Show the 8. Have the students draw this number line as it would look with all the cards turned over.

Have each student make a number line and place all the cards facedown except one. Direct partners to work together:

• Tell your partner how you counted to make your number line.

• Have your partner guess the numbers on other cards as you point to them.

Show a real-world application of

number lines. For example, show a scale, ruler, meterstick, thermometer, clock, graph, and so on. Say a number. Ask the students to indicate where this number would be on the scale. Have them discuss their answers.

Reasoning. Show a number line marked off by tens. Ask:

• Which ten is closest to 43? To 27? To 14? To 35?

Construct another number line with cards. Do not tell the students multiples of which numbers were used. Lead the students in this activity.

• (Turn over one card.) Guess the number to the right of the one shown. Explain your guess.

• (Do not turn over that card yet, but turn over the fourth card to the right of the card that is faceup [see **fig. 3**]). Again guess what number is to the right of the first card. Explain your choice now.

• Repeat these steps until the students have discovered the counting pattern.

Connections. Give each group of students a meterstick and some base-ten metric manipulatives. Ask them questions like these:

• If you start at the end of the meterstick to make a train beside it with 4 tens rods and 3 ones cubes, what number will be at the end of the train? Try it to check.

• How many tens rods and ones cubes would you need to make a train that ended at the number 67? Try it.

• If you put 7 tens rods and 8 ones cubes by the meterstick, will the end of the train be closer to 70 or closer to 80? If you use 2 tens rods and 3 ones cubes? 6 tens rods and 5 ones cubes?

Show a thermometer. Draw a number line to match it. Ask:

• How is the clockface like a number line? Draw what it would look like if it were straight.

5–8 Activities

1. Give pairs of students hundreds and tens manipulatives. Ask them to show 360 and to record the number of hun-

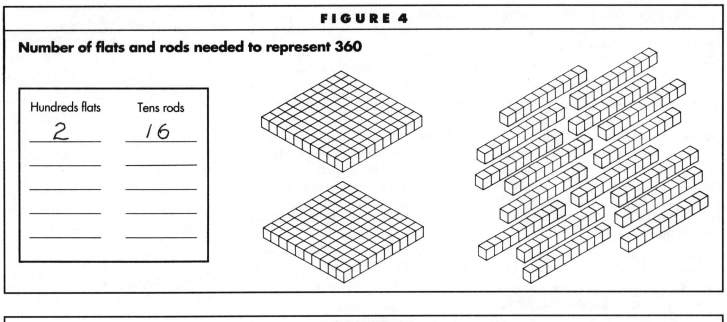

FIGURE 4

Number of flats and rods needed to represent 360

Hundreds flats	Tens rods
2	16

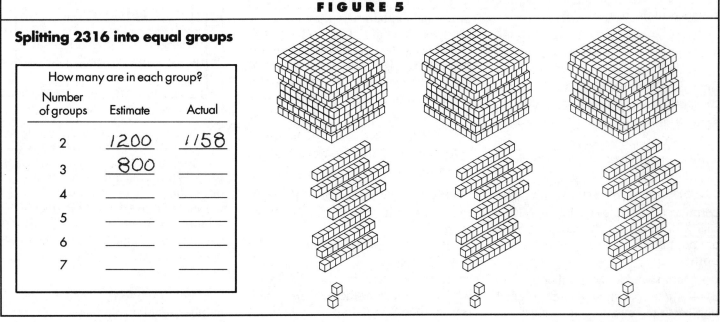

FIGURE 5

Splitting 2316 into equal groups

	How many are in each group?	
Number of groups	Estimate	Actual
2	1200	1158
3	800	
4		
5		
6		
7		

dreds flats and tens rods. Then have them show 360 using fewer flats and again record the number (see **fig. 4**). Students should repeat this activity to find different ways to represent 360.

Problem solving. Ask the students questions like these:

• How many different representations of 360 are possible? Show them all in a table.

• Find another number with the same number of representations as 360. How many numbers have that same number of arrangements?

• How many different representa-tions are possible for 470? Can you find out without making a complete list?

• Find a number that has exactly eight different representations.

Communication. (a) Using □ for hundreds and │ for tens, students should draw all possible arrangements for 240. (b) Have the students explain how four flats and six rods represent the same number as two flats and twenty-six rods.

Reasoning. Ask the following:

• What is the fewest number of blocks (cubes, rods, flats) needed to show 750? What is the greatest number of blocks

that can be used to show 750?

• When you trade a hundred for 10 tens, how does the number of blocks change? Why?

Connections. Ask the students to explain how showing numbers with flats and rods is like using money. Present them with the task of splitting four dollars and two dimes into three piles with equal amounts of money. Ask them questions like these:

• What trades do you have to make?

• Why is it useful to represent num-bers in different ways?

- Write 67 as the sum of two whole numbers; one of the numbers should be a multiple of 10. In how many ways can you do so?

2. Give groups of students base-ten blocks. Have the students use the blocks to split the number 2316 into equal groups in various ways. Before the students trade and rearrange their blocks to illustrate equal groups, have them estimate the number that will be in each group. The students should record their estimates and the actual number in the chart in **figure 5**.

Problem solving. Have students write a problem in which they round 2316 to 2400 then divide by 6. Ask them to explain how many numbers would be rounded to 7200 if all numbers are rounded to the nearest 200.

Communication. Ask students to explain why they might round 4275 to 4300 one time and to 4200 another time. Have students draw base-ten blocks to show how to partition 3200 into eight groups and explain how many are in each group.

Reasoning. Give students problems like these:

- Jerry rounded 5589 to 5400, then partitioned 5400 into equal groups. How many different partitionings of 5400 are possible? List five different possibilities.

- Mary rounded the number 3xxx to 3500, then partitioned the original number into seven equal groups. Explain why you think that the original number was greater than 3149.

Connections. Present the following problems to the students:

- The number of passengers leaving New York for London in one day is 2155. If nine flights leave daily, about how many passengers are on each plane?

- Rauol and Melissa earned $29 by mowing several lawns. Melissa did 3/5 of the work. About how much money should each receive?

3. Give the students a 10 × 10 grid. Have them design the floor plan of an apartment with the following rooms occupying the given percentages of the total floor space (see **fig. 6**):

Living room and kitchen	50 percent
Bedroom	30 percent
Bathroom	16 percent
Storage	4 percent

Problem solving. Ask the students questions like these:

- What fraction of the apartment is the bedroom? Which of the rooms is closest to 0.2 of the apartment?

- If an apartment has only two rooms, what is the percentage of the apartment that the small room can be if the larger room is three times as big? Twice as big? What fraction of the apartment is each room if the larger is three times as big as the smaller? Twice as big?

Communication. Have the students redesign the apartment to suit their tastes and explain why they made the changes they did. Let each student examine the design of a friend and find the room that is closest to one-fourth of the apartment and to 0.4 of the apartment. Each student should discuss with a friend how she or he made these decisions.

Reasoning. Pose questions like the following:

- If you doubled the size of the bathroom, would it be as large as the bedroom?

- If you increase the size of the apartment by 100 percent and all the new space is included in your bedroom, what percentage of the new apartment is each room?

- Suppose that you had an apartment with four rooms. If one room is one-third of the apartment, a second room is one-fourth of the apartment, and a third room is one-fifth of the apartment, about what percentage of the apartment is the fourth room? Order the rooms according to size.

Connections. Give students the following problems:

- Does the chart in **figure 7** account for all the land in Black Hawk County? In what other ways might land be used? Make a circle graph to show how the land is used.

- Scientists surveyed a bird population in George Wythe Park. They found

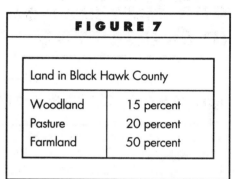

that 25 percent of the birds nested on the ground and 75 percent nested in trees. What is the ratio of the number of birds that nest on the ground to the number of those that nest in trees? Can you write this ratio a different way? If the scientists found 48 birds nesting on the ground, how many birds were surveyed in all?

Many of the foregoing activities on number relationships and representations have been drawn from real-world examples. Teachers can find many other practical examples of similar problems in students' daily lives.

References

Fischer, Florence E. "A Part-Part-Whole Curriculum for Teaching Number in the Kindergarten." *Journal for Research in Mathematics Education* 21 (May 1990): 207-15.

Huinker, DeAnn. "The Effects of Instruction Using Part-Whole Concepts with One-Step and Two-Step Word Problems in Grade Four." Ph.D. diss., University of Michigan, 1990.

Mathison, Kim. "Independent Study: Percent." Unpublished paper written under the direction of Diane Thiessen, University of Northern Iowa, 1987.

National Council of Teachers of Mathematics, Commission on Standards for School Mathematics. *Curriculum and Evaluation Standards for School Mathematics.* Reston, Va.: The Council, 1989.

Number Sense and Numeration in Grades K–8

The K–4 standard focusing on number sense and numeration (NCTM 1989, 38) calls for curricular materials and activities that enable students to—

- construct number meanings through real-world experiences and the use of physical materials;
- understand our numeration system by relating counting, grouping, and place-value concepts;
- develop number sense;
- interpret the multiple uses of numbers in the real world.

The standards for grades 5–8 extend the foregoing ideas to include very large and very small positive and negative numbers and a variety of equivalent representations for numbers, including the use of decimals, exponents, and scientific notation.

The general theme of the standards concerning number sense and numeration is that students need to develop number concepts meaningfully so that they can use numbers effectively in mathematical situations both in and out of school. Students need to use numbers effectively to quantify, identify position, measure, and compute. Further, they need to develop number sense so that they can estimate quantities and determine the reasonableness of proposed solutions to problems involving numbers.

This article discusses the content of the standards focusing on number and numeration in grades K–8. It then describes activities that help students develop sound number concepts and skills in these grades.

Sequence of Development

To develop number meanings throughout grades K–8, numbers should emanate from students' experiences and be carefully linked to physical materials. Initially, numbers should be modeled by using individual counters, such as blocks or craft sticks. These objects are subsequently grouped and counted in various ways to develop concepts and skills associated with place value. By actually grouping objects into sets of ten and grouping sets of ten to make hundreds, students begin to develop the ten-to-one relationship that exists between adjacent place-value positions in our number system. Later, they use pregrouped materials such as base-ten blocks to model numbers involving two, three, or four digits. Symbolic activities should be completed after students have linked the numbers to physical models. Numbers as large as a hundred thousand and a million should be modeled by students so that they can develop a sense of the relative magnitude of these numbers. Negative numbers can be related to real-world ideas, such as temperatures below zero, distances below sea level, and deficits like bank statements and national debts.

Early Concepts of Number and Number Relations

Students' initial concepts of number are based on counting by ones. By counting, students develop concepts of cardinality for numbers and the one-more-than relationship between consecutive numbers. But students benefit from developing a richer understanding of the integrated network of relationships among numbers. They need to relate numbers to the parts that comprise them, relate numbers to the benchmarks of five and ten, develop the idea of the two-more-than relationship, and recognize dot patterns for numbers. An emphasis on developing concepts of number relations in the primary grades enables students to learn the addition and subtraction facts very naturally; they simply record symbolically the relationships between numbers and their component parts that they have already learned.

Edited by **Thomas E. Rowan**
Montgomery County Public Schools
Rockville, MD 20850

Prepared by **Charles S. Thompson**
University of Louisville
Louisville, KY 40292

Chuck Thompson was a member of the K–4 Working Group for the Standards. *He is particularly interested in the use of instructional activities that facilitate children's construction of mathematical concepts and is teaching this year at Moray House College of Education in Edinburgh, Scotland.*

Place-Value Concepts

Place-value concepts are complex and develop slowly over a long period of time. The triangular structure in **figure 1** illustrates relationships among essential place-value concepts. At the top of the triangle are physical models, which may be individual counters or grouped materials like base-ten blocks. On the left side are the oral names used to describe the cardinality of the physical models. On the right side are the symbols used to represent the cardinality of the physical models. In the center of the structure is the student's mental activity as he or she counts the physical models. As the physical models are rearranged, the counting changes accordingly. For example, when individual counters are used, let's say twenty-three of them, the student is likely to count by ones to determine the oral name corresponding to that set of counters. If the counters are grouped by tens, the student will likely count by tens and ones to determine the oral name: ten, twenty, twenty-one, twenty-two, twenty-three. But the student can also count *the number of* tens (two) and ones (three) to link the symbol 23 meaningfully with the objects. The coordination of the various groupings of the physical models with the corresponding ways of counting and with the associated words and symbols is at the heart of students' development of place-value concepts.

Number Sense

Students must develop good number sense so that they can estimate quantities and determine the reasonableness of proposed solutions to problems involving numbers. "Children with good number sense (1) have well-understood number meanings, (2) have developed multiple relationships among numbers, (3) recognize the relative magnitudes of numbers, (4) know the relative effect[s] of operating on numbers, and (5) develop referents for measures of common objects and situations in their environments" (NCTM 1989, 38). The first three of these components are described in the foregoing. The fourth, knowledge of the relative effects of operating on numbers, includes knowing that, for

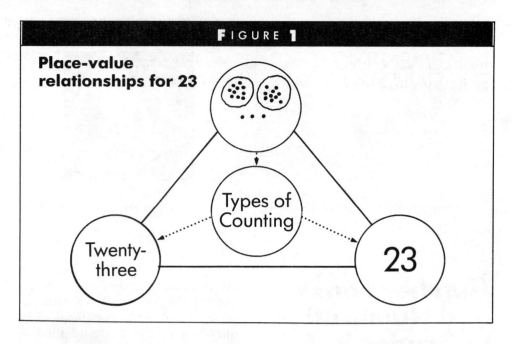

FIGURE 1

Place-value relationships for 23

Types of Counting

Twenty-three

23

example, since 100 + 57 is 157, 98 + 57 is 2 less, or 155. The fifth component includes knowing that, for example, two meters is a reasonable height for a very tall person but that eighty-five students is not a reasonable number to be in a classroom.

Activities for Grades K–4

Number concepts and relations. Hold up some fingers and ask students to hold up the same fingers. Ask them how many they are holding up. Ask them to hold up the same number again, but using different fingers. Repeat, but have them use some fingers on each hand to create the total that you have shown them. Discuss the total shown as composed of the two parts, the fingers on each hand. Continue holding up various sets of fingers, asking them to hold up one more, one less, two more, two less, twice as many, and so on. Flash a set of fingers and see if students can recreate it. Ask them to compare their set of fingers to five fingers, then ten. Continue, asking the students to verbalize their displays and the relationships involved. Increase the number of fingers you hold up as the students become ready.

Counting and place value. Place about ten collections of between twenty and sixty small items on paper plates. Have the students move in groups of three from one collection to the next. At each location they first

count by ones to determine the number of items present, recording the number by using words like *thirty-two*. Then they make as many groups of ten as possible and record the results like this: *3* tens and *2*. Finally, they count by tens and ones and compare this result to the result they obtained when counting by ones. The discussion should focus on the three different types of counts; tell the students the result of one type of count and have them predict the results of the other two, justifying their ideas throughout.

Modeling three-digit numbers. Begin by having students use base-ten cubes (ones), rods (tens), and squares (hundreds) on a three-column mat to model a three-digit number, such as 234. Then, ask them to add (or subtract) 1, 2, or 3; 10, 20, or 30; 100, 200, or 300. Have them verbally justify any trading that is needed each time and the new total, by counting. Then ask questions, such as, "If we trade in all our pieces for tens, how many could we get?" or "Is this number closer to two hundred or three hundred?" or "How many more do we need to get another hundred square?" Continue adding and subtracting quantities as suggested, constantly having students justify their actions and results. After students know the place-value concepts well, put cards labeled with 0–9 at the top of each column to correspond to the number of items in that column. Have students relate these numerals to the quantities represented.

Number sense. Draw a 500-centimeter horizontal segment on the chalkboard. Label the left end 0 and the right end 500. Draw a vertical arrow at some point along the segment and have the students write the numeral that they think should be associated with this arrow. Have students use a meterstick marked in centimeters to determine the correct numeral and write it above the arrow. Continue drawing additional vertical arrows and have the students estimate the corresponding numerals. Focus on the strategies that students use to

0 ←————————↑————————→ 500

determine the numerals. Remember, this is an estimating activity, and all estimates within an acceptable range, say 25 centimeters, are equally good—even estimates that happen to be exact. This activity helps students develop the idea of relative magnitudes of numbers.

Activities for Grades 5–8

Concepts for larger numbers. Line up one centimeter cube (one), one decimeter rod (ten), one decimeter square (hundred), and one decimeter cube (thousand) from right to left. Ask students to verbalize the numerical relationships between adjacent items; use the ten-to-one ratio to determine how the next piece should be built (with 10 thousand-blocks). Have them build this ten-thousand unit by making ten decimeter cubes and connecting them. Repeat for the hundred-thousand unit and the million unit. The million unit will be a cube, one meter on each side **(fig. 2)**. Ask questions that require students to relate the units to one another, for example, "What is the ratio between a million and a thousand? What is the difference between a million and a thousand? How many hundreds in a million?" Note that the ratio between adjacent units is constant, ten to one, but that the difference increases dramatically as the units become larger. The place-value periods are clear in the model (John Van de Walle [pers. com. 1988]).

Reading and writing large numbers. Make use of the preceding ideas and **figure 2** to read and write large numbers. For example, the number 12 045 678 means 12 million-cubes, 45 thousand-cubes, 678 unit cubes. Also, relate exponents to these large numbers. For example, 1 000, which is a thousand cube, has dimensions of $10 \times 10 \times 10$, or 10^3. Likewise, 1 000 000, a million cube, has dimensions of $100 \times 100 \times 100$, or $10^2 \times 10^2 \times 10^2$, which is 10^6. Help students generalize from these examples to any power of 10.

Decimals and number sense. First, have students construct meanings for decimals by linking them with common fractions involving such denominators as 2, 3, 4, 5, 6, 8, 10, and 12. Model the fractions on a unit square divided into 100 equal parts. For example, to model 3/4, shade 3/4 of the unit square, 75 of the 100 parts. Then relate 3/4 to 75/100 and 0.75. Next, present decimals that are not equivalent to familiar fractions, such as 0.7603, and have students approximate those values by relating them to decimal equivalents of familiar fractions. For example, 0.7603 is about 0.76, which is about 0.75, which is about 3/4. Locate fractions and decimals on a number line to help develop

good number sense for these quantities.

Number sense for large numbers. First, solve a problem involving large numbers as a whole-class activity; then, pose several similar problems for students to solve in small groups. The goal is to develop a sense of the relative magnitudes of large numbers by solving interesting problems involving those large numbers. Here is a sample problem: "How long would a string of a million paper clips be?" Actually have students make strings of ten and a hundred paper clips to measure. Use those results and the relationships between numbers to determine the length of a thousand and then a million paper clips. (The answer is about twenty miles!) Relate the results to the distance from school to familiar landmarks. Related problems to solve in small groups might include these: How long are a million footprints (end-to-end)? A million students (holding hands)? A million dollar bills (stacked)? A million students (standing on each other's shoulders)?

Reference

National Council of Teachers of Mathematics. Commission on Standards for School Mathematics. *Curriculum and Evaluation Standards for School Mathematics.* Reston, Va.: The Council, 1989. ▧

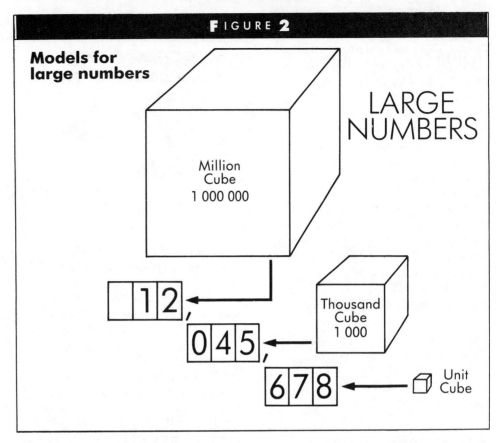

FIGURE 2

Models for large numbers

LARGE NUMBERS

Million Cube 1 000 000

Thousand Cube 1 000

Unit Cube

12, 045, 678

Estimation—Direction from the *Standards*

Do you estimate? Of course you do. Everyone estimates. Research shows that estimation is used in real-world problem solving far more than exact computation. Fur-

Edited by **Thomas E. Rowan**
Montgomery County Public Schools
Rockville, MD 20850

Prepared by **Barbara J. Reys**
and **Robert E. Reys**
University of Missouri at Columbia
Columbia, MO 65211

The Editorial Panel welcomes readers' responses to this article or to any aspect of the Standards.

thermore, estimation relates to every important mathematics concept and skill developed in elementary school. It is a process that allows the user to form an estimate or to judge the reasonableness of a result. The NCTM's *Curriculum and Evaluation Standards for School Mathematics* (*Standards*) (1989) discusses both measurement estimation, for example,

> About how high can you count in one minute?
> About how many beans are in a 1-kg bag **(fig. 1)?**
> Is more than 1/2 the area shaded?

and computational estimation, for example,

> Have you lived 10 000 days?
> I multiplied 48 by 0.27 on my calculator and got 129.6. Can that be right?
> Everything is reduced 35 percent. About how much is saved on the stereo in **figure 2?**

These questions and the discussion of solutions offer many opportunities for developing number sense. Good estimation discussion questions share several common traits. They—

- present a natural problem-solving situation;
- can be solved in a variety of ways, permitting the student freedom in exploring his or her own strategy;
- encourage students to use appropriate computational skills;
- can be used to help teachers better understand students' conceptions

FIGURE 1

Three different processes students use in solving this problem offer insight into not only processes but also misconceptions held by students.

About one million
There are a lot of beans and one million is a big number.

About two thousand
I can hold about one hundred beans in my hand and it will take about twenty handfuls.

About nine hundred
A bean weighs less than one gram, so it would be less than one thousand.

About how many beans are in a 1-kg bag?

FIGURE 2

Three different processes students might use in solving a percentage problem

Fifty percent is one-half; one half of $250 is $125. About $100

Thirty percent of $250 is $75 plus a little. About $80

Thirty-five percent is about one-third; one-third of $240 is $80. About $80

Everything is reduced 35 percent. About how much is saved on the stereo?

$249.49

and misconceptions about numbers;

- furnish an opportunity for communication as students explain the processes and procedures used in making an estimate;
- stimulate different "answers" and therefore offer an opportunity to discuss a range of reasonable answers.

Estimation includes various interrelated concepts and skills, including mental computation, concept development, and number sense. In fact, research suggests that number sense, mental computation, and estimation are often very difficult to separate. Further, the development of any one of these abilities often stimulates further growth in the others.

In the *Standards* estimation is highlighted not as an end in itself but as a means for helping students "develop insights into concepts and procedures, flexibility in working with numbers and measurements, and an awareness of reasonable results" (p. 36). The study of estimation should be integrated with the study of concepts underlying whole numbers, fractions, decimals, and rational numbers so

that these concepts can be constructed meaningfully by the learner. The exploration of a wide range of student-generated estimation strategies is recommended. The use of rounding to estimate is singled out for less attention in the *Standards*. Research and common sense clearly document that traditional rounding rules (rounding to the nearest ten, hundred, thousand, etc.) are often inappropriate and inefficient when estimating. Rather than follow rigid rules for estimating, students should be encouraged to use their knowledge about number to form estimates that are reasonable in the context of the problem. Often this strategy may call for "rounding" to numbers that are more compatible with the computation involved.

Throughout the K–4 and 5–8 sections, the *Standards* strongly endorses systematically developing estimation skills in grades K–8. The specific recommendations are quoted, and several sample activities are used to illustrate the spirit of the recommendations.

In grades K–4, the curriculum should include estimation so that students can—

- explore estimation strategies;
- recognize when an estimate is appropriate;
- determine the reasonableness of results;
- apply estimation in working with quantities, measurement, computation, and problem solving [p. 36].

An Instructional Example

Many varied experiences are needed to develop the concept of relative size of numbers and quantities. Although counting is a useful part of many estimation activities, it is not wise to ask students to estimate things that are easy to count. For example, one would not hold a container of three tennis balls and ask a student to estimate the number of tennis balls. However, one might use the same container filled with different objects for an estimation activity.

Figure 3 shows three containers filled with macaroni, rice, and beans. Students might be asked to decide which container contains the most objects. Would an estimate or an exact count be quicker? Do you need to count the number in each container to decide? Tell why or why not.

Students might be asked to "guess"

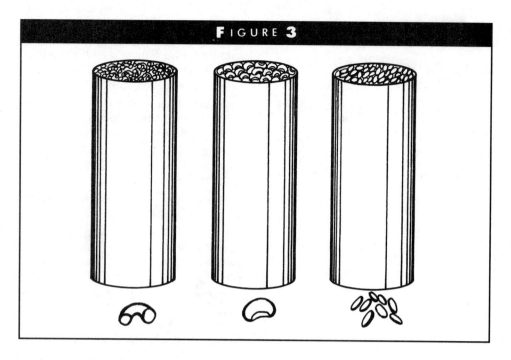

FIGURE 3

For the third exercise a student might think, "Since each number is greater than fifty, the sum must be greater than one hundred." This flexibility of thinking about number and operations is the basis for number sense.

In grades 5–8, the mathematics curriculum should include the development of concepts underlying computation and estimation so that students can—

♦ develop, analyze, and explain procedures for computation and techniques for estimation;
  . . .
♦ select and use an appropriate method for computing from among mental arithmetic, paper-and-pencil, calculator, and computer methods;
♦ use computation, estimation, and proportions to solve problems;
♦ use estimation to check the reasonableness of results.

Whereas much of the focus of estimation in the early grades is on measurement estimation, in grades 5–8 computational estimation should be explored regularly with all operations and with all numbers as soon as the computations get too difficult to do mentally. Just as one does not estimate small quantities, one should avoid estimating computations that can be exactly computed mentally—if possible. Consider the following situation:

Yogurt—425 calories

Orange juice—190 calories

Apple—315 calories

Trail mix—648 calories

If you drink the orange juice and eat the apple, will you consume more than 400 calories? Tell why.

Which two would you eat to total between 900 and 1000 calories?

If you eat each snack listed, will you consume more or less than 2000 calories? Explain your thinking.

Although each of these questions can be answered using exact computation, they can be efficiently and confidently answered by the use of mental computation and estimation. In fact, determining exactly what processes are used is often impossible without asking students to describe what they did. For example, to answer the first question, a student might think, "315

(estimate) the number of items in one container, say, the beans. After all estimates are made, each estimate could be listed from low to high to give students experience in comparing and ordering. Involve all the students in counting the beans by giving each group of two or three students a portion of the beans. Ask them to count their beans and place them in piles of 10. Give the groups plastic bags so that they can put 100 beans into each bag. Ask the whole class to count aloud by 100's, 10's, and 1's to determine the total number of beans.

Once the count is known, review the guesses that were made initially. Which are reasonable? Which are clearly not reasonable? Help students see that several students might have reasonable estimates even though their estimates are different. This knowledge that a range of estimates is acceptable encourages young students to make thoughtful estimates and develop an early tolerance of error, which is an important part of estimation.

This activity can be varied by displaying a container half filled with beans and asking for an estimate of the number of beans. Ask students to tell how they arrived at their estimate. Display their estimates and see if the range of estimates is smaller or larger than in the first activity. Later, ask students to estimate the number of

pieces of macaroni or rice. Check to see how their estimates and strategies are influenced by what they have learned from the bean-estimating activity.

This activity helps students appreciate the power of estimation, develop important mathematical concepts (counting, place value, mental computation, ordering, and comparisons of numbers), develop an early tolerance of error, and participate in problem solving.

The activity we have suggested involves estimation of numerosity. Although in primary grades numbers involved in computations seldom get large enough to require sophisticated estimation strategies, it is important to encourage students to develop benchmarks and understand relative size when computing. When developing two-digit addition techniques this goal might be reached by encouraging students to think about the sum relative to the number 100. For example, in which of the following problems is the sum greater than 100?

14 + 33 + 29   85 + 19   53 + 58

By adding the tens in the first exercise, a student can quickly see that the sum must be less than 100. A student might reason that the second exercise must be more than 100 "because eighty-five plus fifteen is one hundred, and nineteen is more than fifteen."

plus 100 is 415, so the answer must be more than 400.'' Another student more skilled in mental computation might think, ''315 plus 100 is 415 and 90 more is 505, so the answer is more than 400.'' Both are appropriate solutions and illustrate that what was treated as a front-end estimation problem by one student was solved by mental computation by another. As students encounter more tedious computations, the efficiency and power of estimation also increase.

Experiencing and exploring a variety of estimation strategies are essential. Students can get the same estimate for a problem using two or more very different strategies. Different strategies should be illustrated, discussed, and analyzed so that students learn that many different estimation techniques exist. Although no single strategy should be singled out for exclusive use, understanding different strategies will help students make wise decisions about which strategy or strategies are most efficient in a particular situation.

Two Instructional Examples

Students should be encouraged to make sense of all mathematical problems before attempting to solve them. For example, suppose students are exploring multiplication of decimal numbers. The teacher might give them the following set of problems:

489.2 × 0.98	505.33 × 1.08
893 × 0.53	1129 × 0.51
1462 × 0.32	1267.2 × 0.24

Instead of asking students to find the exact answers using paper and pencil or a calculator, focus the discussion on the following questions:

Which of the problems have a product less than 500? Why?

Which have a product greater than 500? Why?

Encourage students to look at each factor and think about its relative size before computing. Help them verbalize the important generalizations they discover. For example, when a num-

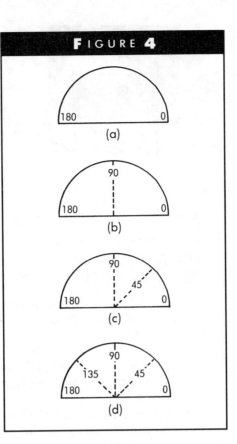

FIGURE 4

(a)

(b)

(c)

(d)

ber is multiplied by a factor less than 1, the product is less than the number. What happens when a number is multiplied by 0.52 or 0.486? How can understanding the relative size of these decimals help in making good estimates?

Students have many opportunities outside of computation to use estimation techniques to help make sense of mathematical problems. Here is an activity that affords an opportunity to estimate before measuring angles with a protractor.

Ask students to make a protractor by cutting a semicircular region out of plain paper **(fig. 4a)**. Fold the region in half, making a slight crease, and mark it as 90 degrees **(fig. 4b)**. Next, fold halfway between the 90-degree mark and the two ends of the diameter of the semicircle and mark the 45-degree spot **(fig. 4c)** and the 135-degree spot **(fig. 4d)**.

Use this protractor to explore a variety of angles in the mathematics text and in the environment. Which angles are less than 45 degrees? Which are between 45 and 90 degrees? Name an angle that is about 135 degrees in measure. About where would an angle of 65 degrees be located on this protrac-

tor? How could you use the protractor to locate a 25-degree angle? Such estimation experiences furnish students with important referents or benchmarks that are invaluable.

As students begin to use the protractor, emphasize the fact that most protractors have two scales—one going from left to right and the other from right to left. Ask how a user knows which scale to use when measuring an angle. Help students realize that having a rough idea of the angle's measure establishes which scale is to be used—only one will show a reasonable measure. For an approach to estimating the size of angles using a computer, see Bitter, Edwards, and Hatfield (1990).

Where to from here?

Much needs to be done to implement the concepts and spirit of teaching estimation portrayed in the *Standards*. Many ideas for helping students develop skills in estimation and mental computation and number sense have been highlighted in several recent NCTM materials, including the 1986 Yearbook, *Estimation and Mental Computation* (Schoen and Zweng 1986); the series "Mental Computation and Estimation" that appeared in the September 1986–May 1987 issues of the *Arithmetic Teacher;* and the special number-sense issue in the February 1989 *Arithmetic Teacher.* Interested readers are invited to contact the authors for a more comprehensive list of other resources that might be useful in bringing about curricular and instructional change in teaching estimation, mental computation, and number sense.

References

Nancy Tanner Edwards, Gary Bitter, and Mary M. Hatfield. "Teaching Mathematics with Technology: Measurement in Geometry with Computers." *Arithmetic Teacher* 37 (February 1990):64–67.

National Council of Teachers of Mathematics, Commission on Standards for School Mathematics. *Curriculum and Evaluation Standards for School Mathematics.* Reston, Va.: The Council, 1989.

Schoen, Harold L., and Marilyn J. Zweng, eds. *Estimation and Mental Computation.* 1986 Yearbook of the National Council of Teachers of Mathematics. Reston, Va.: The Council, 1986. ●

Meanings of Operations

"**C**arlos finally understands subtraction! He got nine of the ten exercises correct, and every one of them involved renaming." Statements like this confuse students' computational proficiency with their understanding of an operation. Ironically, this student's understanding of the operation of subtraction may be very shallow. We often give too little attention to building and assessing concepts of operations, yet this is one of three important components of teaching and learning about number that are included in the NCTM's *Curriculum and Evaluation Standards for School Mathematics* (1989). The first of the three components is the standard on number sense and numeration. Concepts of operations (see **table 1**) is the second and builds on number sense. The third of the three number standards, whole-number computation, must build on the other two areas. A deep understanding of the concepts associated with an operation results from careful attention to many important real-world and mathematical ideas and relationships.

Three broad areas of work are con-

Prepared by **Paul R. Trafton** *and*
  Judith S. Zawojewski
National College of Education
Evanston, IL 60201

Edited by **Thomas E. Rowan**
Montgomery County Public Schools
Rockville, MD 20850

The Editorial Panel welcomes readers' responses to this article or to any aspect of the Standards *for consideration for publication as an article or as a letter in "Readers' Dialogue."*

TABLE 1

 **STANDARD 7:**
CONCEPTS OF WHOLE-NUMBER OPERATIONS

In grades K–4, the mathematics curriculum should include concepts of addition, subtraction, multiplication, and division of whole numbers so that students can—

♦ develop meaning for the operations by modeling and discussing a rich variety of problem situations;

♦ relate the mathematical language and symbolism of operations to problem situations and informal language;

♦ recognize that a wide variety of problem structures can be represented by a single operation;

♦ develop operation sense.

STANDARD 6:
NUMBER SYSTEMS AND NUMBER THEORY

In grades 5–8, the mathematics curriculum should include the study of number systems and number theory so that students can—

♦ understand and appreciate the need for numbers beyond the whole numbers;

♦ develop and use order relations for whole numbers, fractions, decimals, integers, and rational numbers;

♦ extend their understanding of whole-number operations to fractions, decimals, integers, and rational numbers;

♦ understand how the basic arithmetic operations are related to one another;

♦ develop and apply number theory concepts (e.g., primes, factors, and multiples) in real-world and mathematical problem situations.

---

sidered in this article. First, pupils' informal experiences with, and language for, operations need to be linked to the mathematical language and symbolism of an operation. For example, before pupils receive instruction on multiplication or division, they need to be able to solve problems that involve sharing six pennies among three children or putting two cookies on each of four plates. They naturally use such phrases as "come together" or "run away" for addition and subtraction situations. Extended experience in which pupils and teachers share and build a common vocabulary for describing real-world events leads to the use of such words as *part, total,* and *in all.* As pupils act out stories with concrete materials, the information is recorded in a chart. **Figure 1** illustrates this approach for a subtraction situation about having eight pennies and spending five pennies. The rich, concrete language experience is then linked to new vocabulary and eventually to the conventional mathematical language and symbols that represent the story.

Building the mathematical ideas of an operation from real-world problems helps pupils see the many kinds of physical situations associated with an operation. This experience, in turn, better enables them to recognize problem situations to which an operation applies **(fig. 2)** and to understand better the operation in its symbolic form.

The second area of work involves exploring patterns and relationships for an operation, between operations, and between an operation and other mathematical topics (see standard 6 in **table 1**). This work helps students broaden their understanding of an operation and acquire important new understandings. They see, for example, that addition is related to subtraction or that finding one of the three equal parts of a 12 can be expressed as either 1/3 of 12 or 12 ÷ 3. They investigate factors and multiples, which are important aspects of the operation of multiplication, using tiles or graph paper, which leads to ideas about prime numbers (numbers that have exactly two factors) and square numbers (numbers that have an odd number of factors). As students explore patterns, they learn relationships associated with operations and computation involving equal addends or factors.

In addition, for example, when one addend is increased by one and the other addend is decreased by one, the sum remains constant. This relation-

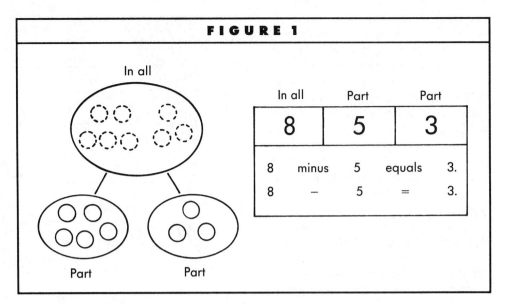

FIGURE 1

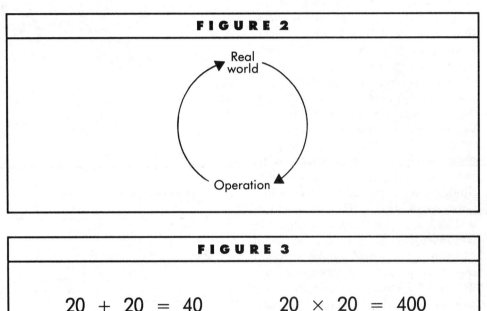

FIGURE 2

FIGURE 3

$$20 + 20 = 40 \qquad 20 \times 20 = 400$$

One more / One less / The same

One more / One less / One less

$$21 + 19 = 40 \qquad 21 \times 19 = 399$$

ship is not true in general for multiplication, but when the two factors are the same and one factor is increased by one and the other factor is decreased by one, the product is one less than the original product (see **fig. 3**). When the factors are not the same the patterns of the products lead to interesting explorations. Explorations with number patterns build familiarity with an operation that goes far beyond the ability to represent a story situation with mathematical symbols. Although work at this level often involves finding answers, the emphasis is not on learning techniques for computing or developing proficiency with facts. Rather, students learn a wide variety of ideas about an operation, their interest in the world of mathematics grows, and their operation sense deepens.

The third area of work with operations is developing a broad understanding of mathematical structure. As students' world of number expands to integers and rational numbers, they experience operations in a wider variety of contexts. They see that the "turn around" for addition (i.e., commutative property) also holds for fractions, decimals, and integers. As they compare and contrast properties as they apply to various sets of numbers, they begin to develop a more general picture of the operations.

Upper-grade students develop underlying concepts of mathematical structure as they examine the characteristics of operations on various sets of numbers. As students resolve perceived "conflicts" between operations on different sets of numbers, they attain a higher level of understanding of that operation. From their work with addition of whole numbers, students develop the idea that, in general, "the sum is more than either addend." Thus, they have difficulty accepting that the *sum* of -4 and $+9$ is $+5$, as it "violates" their perception about addition. The problem seems more like subtraction than addition. Students need to see the connection between addition with whole numbers and addition with integers. In both situations addition is built on the notion of joining. For whole numbers, sets of objects are joined or combined, whereas for integers, distances involving magnitude and direction are combined, such as a four-yard loss combined with a nine-yard gain in football. Students need explicit help to realize that part of their former concept of the operation is still valid but that it is just a part of an enlarged picture of the operation using a new set of numbers. As students achieve this higher level of understanding, they begin to develop an intuitive understanding of mathematical structure.

Careful attention to developing operations on numbers plays an important role in acquiring a rich operation sense that is flexible enough to be expanded and powerful enough for application in a variety of situations. The following activities show additional ways in which students can acquire a thorough understanding of operations of numbers.

FIGURE 4

There were 3 boys. Each of them had 2 markers. How many in all. 3X2=6

Marc C.

Taken from Trafton and Shulte (1989, 196)

FIGURE 5

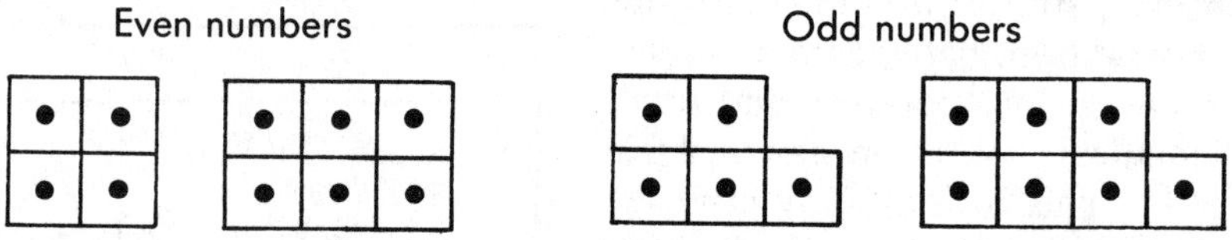

Even numbers   Odd numbers

(a) Odd numbers have one left over.

Names: *Maria   Carlos   Kelly*

5	1	7	7	9	11
+3	+9	+9	+5	+9	+3
8	10	16	12	18	14

We added *two odd numbers.*

We found that *the answer is always even.*

(b) Exploring numerical patterns

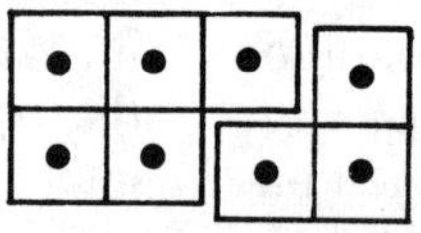

(c) A model showing that the sum of two odd numbers is even

Activities

Developing concepts of operations

Primary-grade pupils need multiple experiences in making connections between familiar situations and an operation. A first-grade class first worked with big-book stories that involved subtraction situations. They talked about sheep running away, rockets blasting off, marbles rolling off tables, and children gobbling up muffins. Then they and their teacher created their own big-book stories. One storybook had a balloon theme. They created and illustrated several stories, including the following:

I went to the circus and I got 10 balloons. And my sister popped 5.

I went to the gift show and saw 7 balloons. My sneaky brother untied 4 of them.

I went to the zoo and I saw 9 purple balloons. My silly cousin blew 2 away.

Other big-book stories also included missing-addend and comparison situations. This work makes use of pupils' language for subtraction situations and builds a smooth transition at a later time for mathematical language and symbolism. The first-grade teacher reported that her pupils made this transition easily and naturally as they built connections together on the basis of the pupils' own stories.

Once pupils have worked with the symbols, they should have many experiences in writing stories for an operation, such as the one shown in **figure 4**.

Exploring patterns and relationships

Many patterns and relationships can be explored and discussed throughout grades K–8. Second- and third-grade pupils can explore patterns for adding odd numbers and even numbers. This work builds on prior physical and pictorial experiences that lead pupils to see that even numbers represent situations in which objects come out even when they are paired, whereas odd numbers represent situations in which one is left over, as shown using dot

cards in **figure 5a**. After pupils explore the numerical patterns, such as the sum of two odd numbers (see **fig. 5b**), a discussion can help them see why the sum of two odd numbers always is an even number, as shown in **figure 5c**. The experience can be extended to generalizations about the

sum of three odd numbers or two even numbers and one odd number. In later grades they can explore patterns for products of odd and even numbers.

In the middle grades characteristics of addition with fractions can be productively discussed using such questions as those shown in **figure 6**.

FIGURE 6

Think about adding two fractions less than one-half.
What is the greatest possible sum? Why?
What is the least possible sum? Why?

Think about adding two fractions less than one.
What is the possible range of sums?

Think about adding two fractions greater than one-half but less than one.
What is the possible range of sums?

Find at least three fractions for each example below that would produce sums (a) greater than one, (b) less than one.

[   ] + ½   [   ] + ¾   [   ] + ⅕   [   ] + ⅝

FIGURE 7

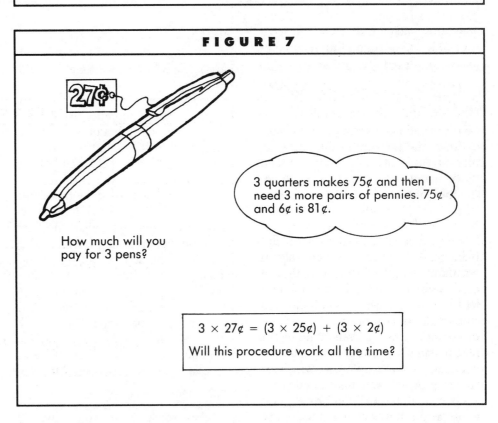

How much will you pay for 3 pens?

3 quarters makes 75¢ and then I need 3 more pairs of pennies. 75¢ and 6¢ is 81¢.

$3 \times 27¢ = (3 \times 25¢) + (3 \times 2¢)$

Will this procedure work all the time?

FIGURE 8

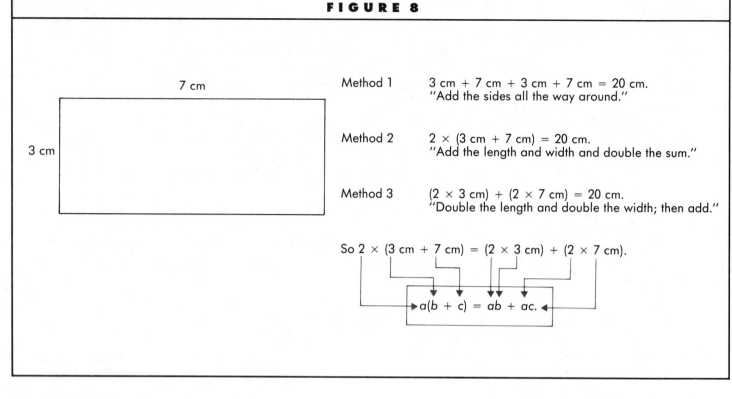

Questions such as this can be used prior to learning computational procedures.

Building understanding of mathematical structure

Students become aware of mathematical structure through examining a variety of situations and activities and "pulling out" the common features. The idea of the distributive property,

$$a(b + c) = ab + ac,$$

is often viewed by teachers as difficult to teach and by students as an isolated fact that has little purpose. Although many students and adults have difficulty with the formal statement and symbolism of this property, they do possess an intuitive understanding of it from using it naturally in a variety of contexts, an example of which is shown in **figure 7**. Thus, initial work needs to connect their informal ideas with the mathematical language and symbolism of the property.

A second situation in which a discussion about this property can arise naturally is finding the perimeter of a rectangle. **Figure 8** shows the kind of thinking that students are likely to share for finding the perimeter of the rectangle. Since each method

"works,"

$$2 \times (3 \text{ cm} + 7 \text{ cm})$$

must equal

$$(2 \times 3 \text{ cm}) + (2 \times 7 \text{ cm}).$$

The symbolic statements usually are given as verbal statements, such as, "First double the length of the long side; next, double the length of the short side; then add the two numbers you get," which are then translated into symbols. The two symbolic statements make sense because they are based on concrete experiences that yield the same solution. This experience can then be the basis for a more direct focus on the distributive property. The work can be generalized by representing length and width by a and b and having both verbal and symbolic statements. When students arrive at the general statement

$$2(a + b) = 2a + 2b,$$

it makes sense to them because of their direct experience with the situation from which it arose and the fact that the symbolic statement is merely a shorthand version of their verbal descriptions. This experience also links numerical, geometric, and algebraic representations of the same idea, which contributes to students' seeing

mathematics as an integrated whole.

Summary

Helping students build more complete concepts of operations can present many opportunities to explore and link many aspects of mathematics. By posing situations that are grounded in concrete experiences that are relevant to students, we can help students see the commonalities that occur across contexts—commonalities that are represented by the language and symbolism of mathematics. Experiences that expand and enrich concepts of addition, subtraction, multiplication, and division help students develop mathematical power through understanding mathematical ideas and gain confidence in their ability to investigate new ideas and attack nonroutine problems.

References

National Council of Teachers of Mathematics, Commission on Standards for School Mathematics. *Curriculum and Evaluation Standards for School Mathematics*. Reston, Va.: The Council, 1989.

Trafton, Paul R., and Albert P. Shulte, eds. *New Directions for Elementary School Mathematics*. 1989 Yearbook of the National Council of Teachers of Mathematics. Reston, Va.: The Council, 1989. ♥

IMPLEMENTING THE *STANDARDS*

Redefining Computation

Pencil-and-paper computational skills have long dominated the elementary school curriculum. For over ten years we have been hearing that the emphasis on these skills must be reduced because in our technological society they are much less important than in previous times. Furthermore, a valid, frequently voiced argument suggests that the time spent on computation is the one "fat" area where cuts can be made to allow time for the many new concepts and higher-order processes that are more important.

Ironically, the *Curriculum and Evaluation Standards for School Mathematics* (*Standards*) (NCTM 1989) actually calls for a *broadening* of the treatment of computation in school mathematics, not a reduction. This notion of doing more and better with computation, not less, is directly on target for a mathematics curriculum of the 1990s. It is also an expedient political view to take when advocating change. As Coburn (1989) points out, "reform will not come smoothly. . . . The public will be skeptical about any proposals for de-emphasizing computation" (p. 43).

The K–4 standard on computation

Prepared by **John A. Van de Walle**
Virginia Commonwealth University
Richmond, VA 23284

Edited by **Thomas E. Rowan**
Montgomery County Public Schools
Rockville, MD 20850

The Editorial Panel welcomes readers' responses to this article or to any aspect of the Standards *for consideration for publication as an article or as a letter in "Readers' Dialogue."*

(see **fig. 1**) addresses only whole-number computation. The areas of estimation, number sense and numeration, and fractional and decimal concepts are dealt with in separate standards. These issues are so closely related, however, that they cannot be ignored when discussing computation, as is stressed in the standard on connections. The corresponding 5–8 standard (see **fig. 1**) is titled "Computation and Estimation" and includes computation with whole numbers, fractions, decimals, percents, proportions, and integers. This standard calls for the inclusion of mental computation and estimation and the use of calculators and computers. The following statements represent a synthesis of the points that are made at both levels:

• Mastery of the basic facts for all operations is essential. Conceptually based thinking strategies should be used to help students master facts, relate them to each other, and apply them to other situations

• Computational-estimation techniques should be developed in a flexible atmosphere. The value of computational estimation, knowing when an estimate is appropriate, and the use of estimates in real-world situations should all be significant parts of the computation curriculum.

• Mental-computation techniques should be developed in a similarly flexible atmosphere as that for estimation. It should encourage flexibility and the use of a wide variety of student-invented procedures.

• Calculators should be a readily available method of computation for students at all levels just as they are for adults in the real world. Students

FIGURE 1

The computation standards for grades K–4 and 5–8

STANDARD 8: WHOLE NUMBER COMPUTATION

In grades K–4, the mathematics curriculum should develop whole number computation so that students can—

♦ model, explain, and develop reasonable proficiency with basic facts and algorithms;

♦ use a variety of mental computation and estimation techniques;

♦ use calculators in appropriate computational situations;

♦ select and use computation techniques appropriate to specific problems and determine whether the results are reasonable.

STANDARD 7: COMPUTATION AND ESTIMATION

In grades 5–8, the mathematics curriculum should develop the concepts underlying computation and estimation in various contexts so that students can—

♦ compute with whole numbers, fractions, decimals, integers, and rational numbers;

♦ develop, analyze, and explain procedures for computation and techniques for estimation;

♦ develop, analyze, and explain methods for solving proportions;

♦ select and use an appropriate method for computing from among mental arithmetic, paper-and-pencil, calculator, and computer methods;

♦ use computation, estimation, and proportions to solve problems;

♦ use estimation to check the reasonableness of results.

From *Curriculum and Evaluation Standards for School Mathematics* (NCTM 1989)

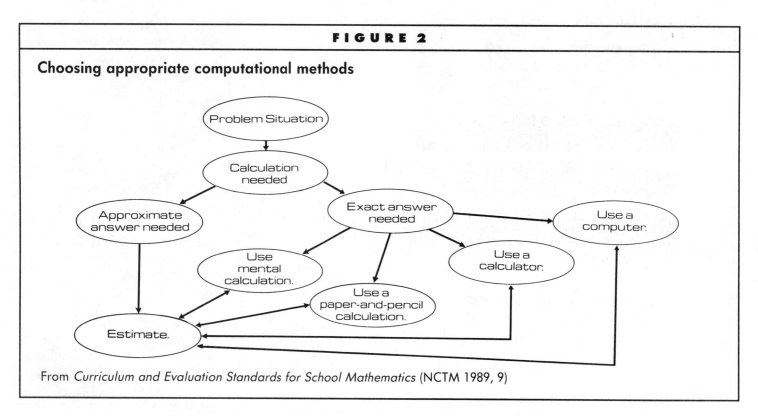

FIGURE 2

Choosing appropriate computational methods

From *Curriculum and Evaluation Standards for School Mathematics* (NCTM 1989, 9)

should learn when the calculator is appropriate as a means of computation and should use estimates to be alert to easily made calculator errors.

• Computation with pencil and paper should still be taught. Students should be encouraged to use manipulatives to explain the rationale for each algorithm. The emphasis should be placed on the conceptual development of the algorithms. Problems should largely be limited to those that can be explored with models, with excessively tedious exercises eliminated. Drill to develop speed and efficiency is much less important than formerly thought.

• Students should explore the value of computers for appropriate applications, such as repetitious computations made on a long list of numbers or computations involving repeated applications of complex formulas. Spreadsheets lend themselves especially well to such computations and are well within the grasp of middle-grade students.

The *Standards*'s vision of computation thus represents a broadening of the curriculum to include mental computation, computational estimation, and the use of technology. Such a broadened view also suggests that

making appropriate choices of computational methods must be part of the curriculum (see **fig. 2**). If calculators are on students' desks every day from early grades onward, the choice of calculator versus mental computation, pencil and paper, or estimation is an everyday issue. Students will learn these choices by living with them.

For children to be actively engaged in developing alternative, efficient methods of computation requires an understanding of numbers, numeration systems, and meanings of operations. The explorations that build on these concepts will serve to strengthen them. "Premature expectations for students' mastery of computational procedures not only cause poor initial learning and poor retention but also require that large amounts of instructional time be spent on teaching and reteaching basic skills" (NCTM 1989, 46).

Activities for Grades K–4

Computation as broadly defined in the *Standards* can begin as early as kindergarten through activities that focus on numerical relationships and combinations of numbers.

Building numbers

Select a single number, for example, 8. Give students different materials with which to "build" 8 in two or three parts. They might use several colors of cubes to build rows of eight; use toothpicks, shells, or patterning blocks to build designs with eight elements; or find combinations for 8 from dot cards or ordinary playing cards. Have students say a two- or three-part number sentence to go with each design or combination (see **fig. 3**).

Basic facts

Much has been written about using thinking strategies to master basic facts, an approach clearly emphasized by the *Standards*. It is important to let the students develop these ideas by building on relationships that are meaningful to them. In **figure 4**, a ten-frame model for the problem 8 + 6 might lead to several different ways of thinking about this combination.

Incredible equations

In *Box It or Bag It Mathematics* (Burk, Snider, and Symonds 1988), students create "incredible equations" each day as ways to express the day of the month. The open-ended atmosphere of the activity encourages

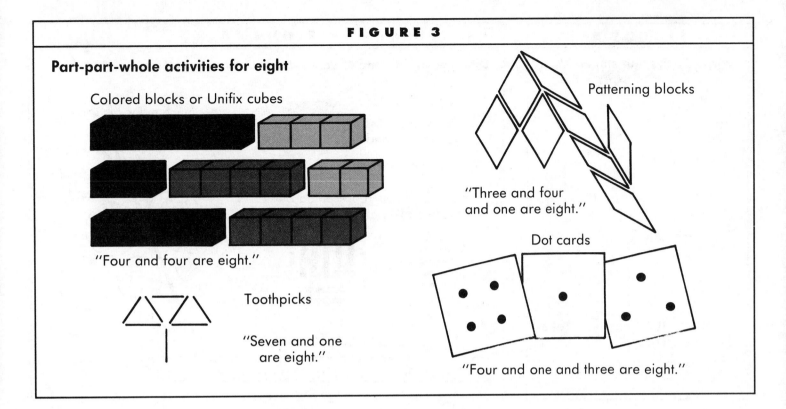

FIGURE 3

Part-part-whole activities for eight

Colored blocks or Unifix cubes

Patterning blocks

"Three and four and one are eight."

Dot cards

"Four and four are eight."

Toothpicks

"Seven and one are eight."

"Four and one and three are eight."

FIGURE 4

Flexible thinking about basic facts

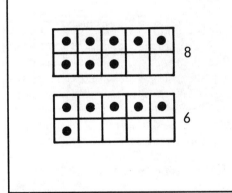

8

6

a) If I move 1 counter down, then 8 + 6 is double 7, or 14.

b) If I remove 2 from the 6 and make the 8 into 10, then it's just 10 and 4, or 14.

c) I think of taking 5 from each to make 10. Then 3 and 1 are 4. That's 14.

d) Double 6 is 12. Then there are 2 more in the 8. So 12 and 2 are 14.

students to search for more and more creative expressions, as shown in **figure 5** (Howden 1989).

Inventing ways to add

Consider the sum 48 + 76. The four approaches illustrated in **figure 6** could be explored in grades 1 to 3, each on different days. The idea is to use different stimuli to encourage the construction of alternative procedures and relationships. No one way is "right," and teachers do not need to stress or even show students the standard procedure.

a) Students make each number with base-ten materials in two piles. Usually the tens will be combined first, with assorted methods used to complete the sum.

b) Show coins for the two amounts on the overhead projector or draw them on the chalkboard.

c) Tape two metersticks end to end on the chalkboard to create a number line for the numbers 0 to 200. If you start with 48 will you use a different strategy than if you begin with 76? How are these methods like the coins or different from using the base-ten models?

d) Write the two numbers on the chalkboard in the usual manner for computation and let students use and explain whatever methods they want to get the sum but have them compute the sum mentally. This approach is especially appropriate for students who have not been taught the standard pencil-and-paper procedure.

These same approaches can be used for subtraction, for such products as 73 × 5 (illustrate only the 73 with coins, base-ten pieces, or on the number line), and for division by a number less than 10 (again, model only the dividend).

The actual numbers in exercises such as these can be adjusted for different grade levels. For example, second-grade students can learn to add a one-digit number to a two- or three-digit number mentally through similar activities.

Quick estimates

Since young students have difficulty with the concept of an estimated computation, one idea is to ask them to judge if a computation is more or less than a given number. This approach initially avoids the need to come up with a specific estimate and can later lead to discussions of different spe-

FIGURE 6

Different stimuli tend to cause different thought patterns.

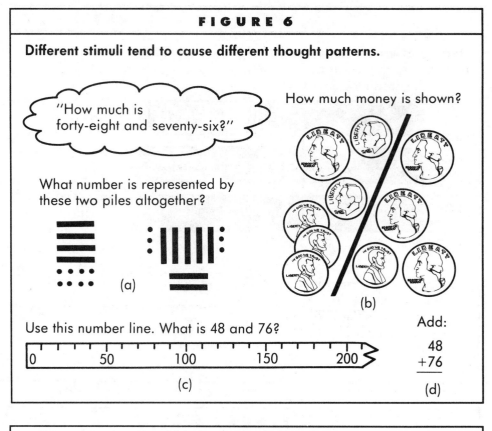

"How much is forty-eight and seventy-six?"

How much money is shown?

What number is represented by these two piles altogether?

(a)

(b)

Use this number line. What is 48 and 76?

(c)

Add:

48
+76

(d)

FIGURE 7

Students think of ¾ of 1⅔ in different ways.

¾ of 1 whole is ¾. Then divide the ⅔ into 4 parts. Those parts are sixths of the whole, so we have ¾ and ³⁄₆, or ¾ + ½.

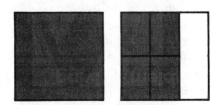

$$\frac{1}{2} + \frac{1}{4} + \frac{1}{2} = 1\frac{1}{4}$$

You get ¾ of 1; then ¾ of each of the thirds pieces is ³⁄₁₂ of each piece. That's ⁶⁄₁₂, or ½. And ¾ plus ½ is 1¼.

We figured that 1⅔ was ⁵⁄₃. So we divided each thirds piece into 4 small pieces and took 3 of them from each. That makes 15 pieces in all. Then we figured that there are 12 little pieces in one whole square. So that means the little pieces are twelfths—¹⁵⁄₁₂.

cific estimates and how students arrived at them. For example, is 482 + 129 + 68 more or less than 800? More or less than 600? A similar but more challenging task is to place the estimated computation in one of several intervals. For example, is 29 × 6 less than 200, between 200 and 300, or more than 300? The targets or intervals can be written on the chalkboard and a short series of computations prepared for the same choices.

Activities for Grades 5–8

The authors of the 5–8 standard on computation and estimation note that "computation, estimation, or methods of solving proportions should not be considered or taught as ends in themselves . . . [but] should be integrated with the study of the concepts underlying fractions, decimals, integers, and rational numbers" (p. 94). The following activities are intended to illustrate this aspect of the *Standards*.

Fraction products

Challenge students to do a computation before they are taught the usual algorithm. For example, have stu-

dents use drawings or materials to explain how to find ¾ of 1⅔. Suggest that a square might be a good model for one whole. Allow students to work in pairs or small groups and put the emphasis on developing a good expla-

nation. As shown in **figure 7**, not all explanations will be the same.

Percentages as fractions

If such simple fractions as halves, thirds, fourths, fifths, and eighths are

FIGURE 8

Students explain their strategies for finding solutions to problems involving fraction concepts.

If brown (8) is one whole, find ¾. Find 1¼.

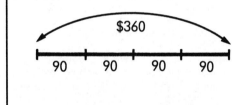

Red rods are fourths. So count fourths. *Three*-fourths is the same as a dark green. Next, 1¼ is *five*-fourths. 1¼ is the orange rod (10).

Draw a line segment. Call it ⅗. Then draw another line segment that's as long as one whole.

$$\frac{3}{5}$$

First, divide the line into 3 parts. Since this is ⅗, each part is ⅕ (one-fifth, two-fifths, three-fifths).

$$\frac{3}{5}$$

$$1.$$

Then count on two more fifths to make a whole.

FIGURE 9

A student explains the use of fraction concepts to solve percentage problems.

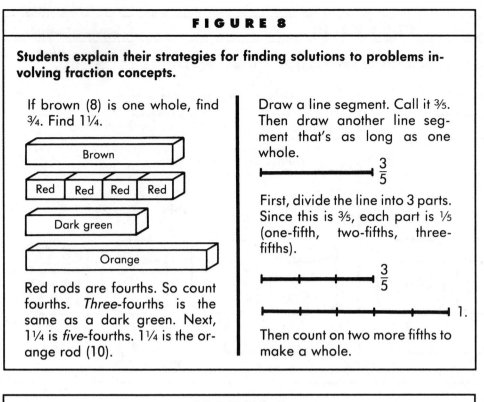

20% is *one*-fifth, so the $360 is the other *four*-fifths. Divide the $360 into four parts—$90 in each part. Then *one*-fifth is $90, and so one more fifth would be the whole. Thus $90 + $360 = $450.

connected with decimal and percentage concepts, the same mental methods can be used to work in each of these domains.

Students can use line segments or Cuisenaire rods to explore problems like those shown in **figure 8**. These same techniques can then be used to solve such problems as the following:

STEREO
20% OFF
You pay only
$360

What was the original price of the stereo?

Figure 9 illustrates a solution.

Similarly, in the following problem, an estimate can be made by using a "close" percentage with a useful fractional equivalent.

The treasurer reported that 68.3% of the dues had been collected for a total of $385. How much more money could the club expect to collect if all the dues are paid?

Here the numbers are not "nice." But if students recognize that 68.3 percent is close to ⅔ (about 67%), then the $385 is ⅔. If $385 is *two*-thirds, then about $190 (half of $380) is *one*-third, which is a bit less than the additional amount the club can expect. Students should still be asked to sketch a simple fraction model, such as a line segment or a square, to justify their reasoning.

Solving proportions

The tasks in **figure 10** require students to use counters or strips to determine the missing parts so that the

ratios in each pair are the same. Notice that in **figures 10a** and **10c** a unit ratio is easily seen *within* the first of two pairs. (Both are in a 1-to-3 ratio.) This ratio can then be used to find the long rod or the number of dark counters in the second pair of each example. In **figures 10b** and **10d**, the unit ratio is not obvious because that ratio is not a whole number. However, if comparisons are made *between* corresponding parts of the two pairs, a whole-number common factor can be used to determine the missing part.

Problems such as these can be posed with line segments, Cuisenaire rods, bars of Unifix cubes, or sets of counters in two colors. The solution methods should come from groups of students as they develop and share with others their own procedures.

Next consider the following two problems:

Tamara bought 3 widgets for $2.40. At the same price, how much would 10 widgets cost?

Tamara bought 4 widgets for $3.75. At the same price, how much would a dozen widgets cost?

Ask students to draw pictures to explain their solutions. In the first of these problems, the unit ratio (within) is easy to figure out mentally ($0.80 per widget). In the second, the common factor (between) is easier to use (one dozen is 3 times as many).

The point is that students can reason proportionally and solve proportions without setting up equations and using a cross-product approach. The word problems are preceded by similar tasks involving models. Then the numbers in the problems are selected so that the same types of reasoning can be used but without tedious computation. Later, students can use these explorations as a basis on which to build solutions to problems that do not work out as nicely. Consider the following example:

Apples are 3 pounds for $0.79. How much would you pay for 5 pounds?

A reasonable method of attacking this problem is to estimate by rounding $0.79 to $0.75 to get a unit ratio of $0.25, giving the answer of a little

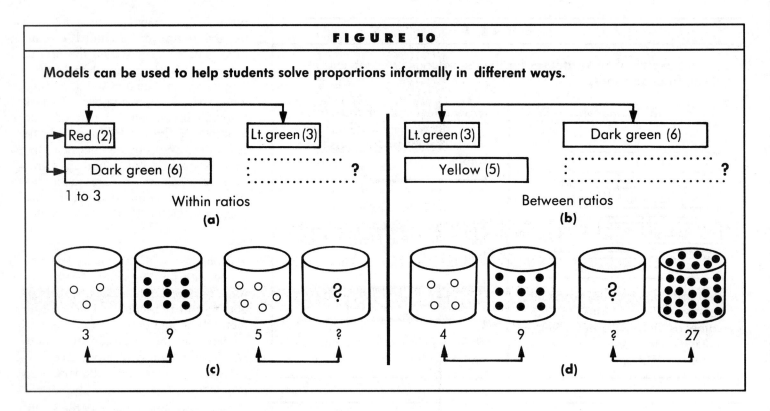

FIGURE 10

Models can be used to help students solve proportions informally in different ways.

1 to 3

Within ratios

(a)

Between ratios

(b)

(c)

(d)

more than $1.25, or maybe $1.30. However, if students wanted an exact result, several equivalent proportions can be established using the same thinking that was used earlier. The *between* ratios are 3/5 and 79/*x*. Alternatively, the *within* ratios are 3/79 and 5/*x*. Equating either pair of ratios yields the same solution.

Conclusion

Yes, the *Standards* calls for more computation than ever before. But the tedious, drill-oriented, rule-driven, pencil-and-paper emphasis should be substantially decreased. Instead, computation in the world of technology has many facets. It is intricately tied to conceptual understanding of numbers and operations. It is flexible, having many different forms and even different procedures within these forms. This broadened view of computation offers new challenges and new excitement for an interactive, dynamic approach to teaching, learning, and students' empowerment.

References

Burk, Donna, Allyn Snider, and Paula Sy-

monds. *Box It or Bag It Mathematics*. Salem. Oreg.: Math Learning Center, 1988.

Coburn, Terrence E. "The Role of Computation in the Changing Mathematics Curricu- *School Mathematics*, 1989 Yearbook of the National Council of Teachers of Mathematics, edited by Paul R. Trafton and Albert P. Shulte, 43–56. Reston. Va.: The Council. 1989.

Howden, Hilde. "Teaching Number Sense." *Arithmetic Teacher* 36 (February 1989):6–11.

National Council of Teachers of Mathematics. Commission on Standards for School Mathematics. *Curriculum and Evaluation Standards for School Mathematics*. Reston. Va.: The Council. 1989. ♥

Implications of NCTM's *Standards* for Teaching Fractions and Decimals

FIGURE 1

Representations of one-fourth

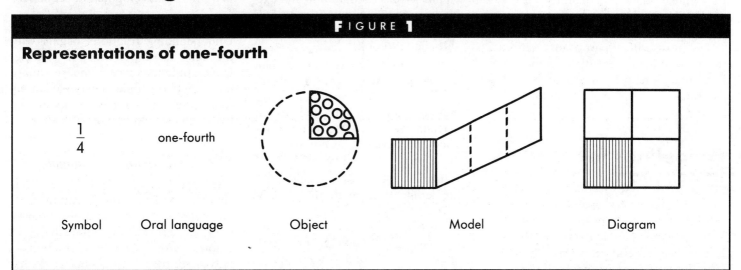

$\frac{1}{4}$ one-fourth

Symbol   Oral language   Object   Model   Diagram

A second grader calls all parts "half," no matter how large they are. A fourth grader writes 3.10 as the decimal for 3/10. A sixth grader can compute 1/2 × 1/2 but cannot reason that one-half of one-half of a pizza is one-fourth of the whole. Most eighth graders cannot estimate the sum 7/8 + 12/13 from choices of 1, 2, 19, and 21. Classroom teachers easily recognize similar deficiencies and ask, How do I teach for greater success?

Edited by **Thomas E. Rowan**
Montgomery County Public Schools
Rockville, MD 20850

Prepared by **Joseph N. Payne**
University of Michigan
Ann Arbor, MI 48109

Ann E. Towsley
University of Michigan—Flint
Flint, MI 48502

The Editorial Panel welcomes readers' responses to this article or to any aspect of the Standards.

The NCTM's *Curriculum and Evaluation Standards for School Mathematics (Standards)* (1989) speak with clarity about a sensible instructional approach, an approach also well supported by many research studies. The K–4 standards emphasize concepts, number sense, models, applications, and exploration of operations (p. 75). Standards for 5–8 include a variety of equivalent forms for numbers and number sense (p. 87), as well as concepts underlying computation and estimation (p. 94). The communication standards (pp. 26, 78) include relations between and among physical materials, pictures, diagrams, and oral and written symbols. Problem solving is the first standard for both K–4 and 5–8 (pp. 23, 75).

The *Standards* suggests a classroom in which mathematics activities arise from familiar problem situations and in which students cooperatively assess and solve problems, apply their

critical-thinking skills, and communicate with each other as they compare strategies and explain reasoning. The *Standards* suggests a classroom in which the teacher makes explicit the connections between mathematical topics, for instance, showing how the same concept is used for decimal as for whole-number addition—likes are added to likes (e.g., tenths to tenths and hundredths to hundredths).

In general, the goals reflect the establishment of a rich conceptual foundation in the primary grades and the building of meaningful computational procedures in the middle and upper grades.

Conceptualization

Knowledge that is stored in memory with many connections to ideas and experiences is conceptual in nature. For fractions and decimals, it requires strong connections between and among the items in **figure 1.** For example, a fifth grader could not show six-thirds of a candy bar until the teacher asked him to say it out loud. When he said "six thirds," he knew what to do. The oral language made him think of the concrete representation.

Comparison and estimation enrich conceptual knowledge because they require students to use the quantity the symbol represents. They must judge the quantity in relation to another quantity, for example, in comparing 2/10 and 2/3. In estimation, they must relate the quantity represented by the fraction to ones easily recognized, such as 0, 1, 1/2, or 1/4.

The most critical part of instruction in fractions is the careful development of sound concepts of fractions and decimals prior to any computational work.

Guidelines for Instruction

On the basis of NCTM's *Standards*, our research, the research of others, and our own teaching experience, we offer these general guidelines for instruction in fractions and decimals.

1. Allocate more instructional time to the development of concepts of the numbers, including more time using concrete materials at all levels. At least two weeks are needed in each grade K–4 and a full week each for fractions and decimals in each grade 5–8, plus regular maintenance.

2. Allocate more time to initial instruction in operations, making good connections between models and algorithms. Several days for each operation are required for sound instruction.

3. Make major adaptations to textbooks. No current textbook includes sufficient developmental work on concepts, and by the nature of the print media, textbooks do not contain oral language and real objects. Inadequate conceptual development is especially noticeable in the middle- and upper-grade texts. With the heavy

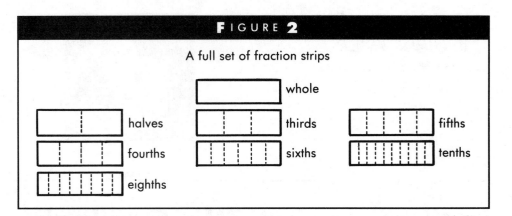

FIGURE 2

A full set of fraction strips

halves | whole
fourths | thirds | fifths
eighths | sixths | tenths

emphasis on computation in textbooks, expect to spend up to half the instructional time working outside the textbook.

4. View computation as broader than paper-and-pencil algorithms. Computation includes mental arithmetic, estimation, and the use of calculators—all as tools to be applied appropriately to complex applications and problem solving.

5. Infuse problem solving and real-life applications with the experiences of students. Help students see the usefulness of fractions and decimals for solving problems apart from school and textbooks.

6. Limit the complexity of computation, especially for addition and subtraction with unwieldy fractions and mixed numbers. Operations with complicated mixed numbers are neither very practical nor essential for further study of mathematics. The new objectives in Michigan, for example, severely limit mixed-number work and the size of the denominators, emphasizing instead related fractions that are useful—halves, fourths, and eighths; thirds and sixths; and fifths and tenths.

Suggestions that are more specific for the levels K–4 and 5–8 follow.

Fractions and Decimals, K–4

In K–4 the work should be mostly oral (only oral in K–2), using models and realistic problems. The following

is a proved developmental sequence.

1. *Sharing and equal-sized pieces*

Understanding fractions begins with the familiar experience of sharing. Have students share a cheese square between two people, a clay pie among four plates, or a set of books among five shelves. Emphasize "fair shares" and "equal parts."

2. *Part and whole—oral language*

Use precise terms for the "fair shares," or fractions. Partition obvious wholes, such as apples, candy bars, or circles, and name parts of wholes with "friendly" fractions—halves, thirds, fourths, fifths, sixths, eighths, and tenths; in K–2, halves, thirds, fourths, and tenths are sufficient.

Third and fourth graders can make their own full set of fraction strips by folding unit strips (2 in. by 8 1/2 in.). They can be stored in an envelope for future use. The teacher may have to mark thirds and fifths. See **figure 2.**

Count. Students count forward and backward, showing the pieces of the fraction strips as they count ("zero thirds, one third, two thirds, three thirds, four thirds . . ."). Students pair up to show fractions over one.

Show. As you say names of fractions, such as "one-fourth" or "two-halves," students show them with their fraction strips. Then show fractional parts and have students give the names. Have them show parts of various shapes—"If this sheet of paper is a whole, then show me one-fourth of it."

Realistic problems. Use such common objects as pizzas, fruit, and sandwiches to share and to name fractional parts.

3. Comparisons—oral language

Use fraction strips to compare fractions represented by single pieces ("Which is more, one-tenth or one-fourth? Why does a tenth sound bigger?"), the same number of pieces of different sizes (two-thirds and two-tenths), more than one piece of the same size (two-fourths and three-fourths), and finally different numbers of pieces of different sizes (one-fifth and six-tenths).

4. Equivalence, estimation, and comparisons—oral language

Use fraction strips to help students fill in the charts, first for zero and one and later for one-half. Find and describe patterns ("close to one if the first number is close to the second number," etc.). See **figure 3**. Make such comparisons as two-fourths with five-tenths, nine-tenths with four-eighths, and three-sixths with one-fourth.

5. Fraction symbols

Relate terms to symbols (two-thirds—2/3, ten-eighths—10/8, eight-tenths—8/10), then write fractions and have students read them. Include halves because 3/2 is often read as "three twos."

Use models and realistic problems. Have students partition and shade figures and write fractions for parts **(fig. 4)**.

6. Decimal concepts—oral language

Use the tenths strips and base-ten blocks as models for decimals.

Count. "Zero tenths, one tenth, two tenths, . . ."

Show. Four-tenths, seven-tenths, twelve-tenths.

Compare. "Which is more—two-tenths or six-tenths?"

Equivalents. "How many tenths make one whole? One-half?"

7. Decimal symbols

Show that fractions for tenths can be written with two different symbols,

with "tenths" hidden in 0.3. Practice matching decimals, models, and fractions **(fig. 5)**. Decimals for tenths are taught easily in grade 3 after steps 1–5.

8. Operations—exploration

Use fraction strips to add and subtract with like fractions. "Kelsey, hold up three-eighths. Ryan, hold up two-eighths **(fig. 6)**. How much do you both have together? How much more does Kelsey have than Ryan?" Extend the ideas using related fractions, such as fourths and halves.

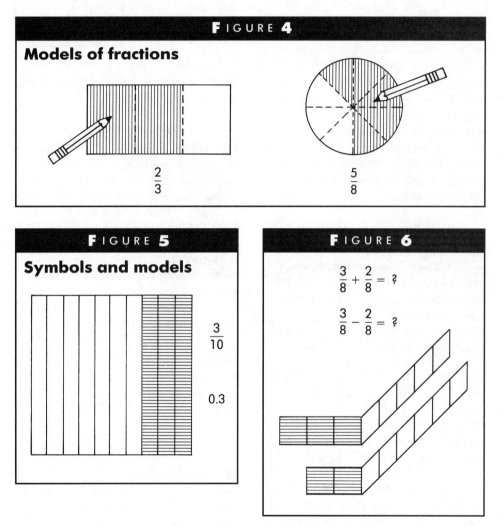

FIGURE **3**

Equivalence and estimation

Zero	Close to zero		One	Close to one		One-half
0 tenths	1 tenth		10 tenths	9 tenths		5 tenths
0 sixths	1 sixth		8 eighths	7 eighths		3 sixths
0 fifths	1 fifth		4 fourths	3 fourths		4 eighths

FIGURE **4**

Models of fractions

$$\frac{2}{3}$$

$$\frac{5}{8}$$

FIGURE **5**

Symbols and models

$$\frac{3}{10}$$

0.3

FIGURE **6**

$$\frac{3}{8} + \frac{2}{8} = ?$$

$$\frac{3}{8} - \frac{2}{8} = ?$$

Fractions and Decimals, 5–8

All work should begin with concrete models, realistic problems, and oral language. Decimals could begin after step 4.

1. Fraction concepts

Use steps 1–5 for grades K–4 to redevelop meanings using regions and objects. Extend to the more difficult linear and set models, emphasizing the whole.

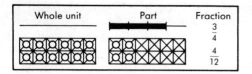

Whole unit	Part	Fraction
		$\frac{3}{4}$
		$\frac{4}{12}$

Use a variety of shapes to make a whole, given a part. "If the piece is one-sixth, then what is the whole?" Sample answers:

2. Equivalence—objects and models

Explore equivalence. "Write fractions for one-half a candy bar, a whole pizza cut into equal pieces, the number one." Show doubling of numerator and denominator with fraction strips. The ideas of multiplying and dividing by any number can be developed over time.

3. Different names for fractions

Extend ideas of equivalent fractions with fraction strips and diagrams, giving special attention to mixed numbers and fractions greater than one. "Draw two and one-fourth using wholes and then using only fractions. How do you write each?" (2 1/4, 9/4) "Write ten-fourths as many ways as you can and draw diagrams to prove your answer." (2 2/4, 1 6/4, 2 1/2, 1 3/2, 2 4/8, . . .)

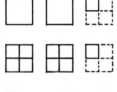

Encourage the use of fractions equivalent to one instead of formal rules. "Ten-fourths is four-fourths and four-fourths and two-fourths—two wholes and two fourths."

4. Estimation and comparison

Extend the K–4 charts to include close to 1/2, 1/4, and 1/3. Find and describe patterns.

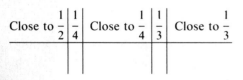

Close to $\frac{1}{2}$	$\frac{1}{4}$	Close to $\frac{1}{4}$	$\frac{1}{3}$	Close to $\frac{1}{3}$

Make comparisons, as with 5/9 and 3/7 (5/9 > 1/2; 3/7 < 1/2).

5. Operations—explorations

Practical problems for all operations can and should be used prior to the introduction of algorithms.

Multiplication. "Juanita has one-half of a pizza. She gives one-third of it to Rebecca. How much does Rebecca get?"

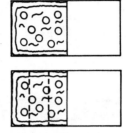

Division. "Steve divides three candy bars into fourths. How many fourths does he get?"

6. Operations—algorithms

Use practical problems and diagrams to develop and illustrate algorithms. "What does 6 ÷ 1/4 ask?" (How many quarter pizzas are in six whole pizzas?) "How do you find that number?" (Multiply 6 by 4.)

After developing and practicing algorithms, revisit the original models with diagrams or fraction strips to confirm answers.

7. Decimals—concepts

Use base-ten blocks, naming hundredths first as "tenths and hundredths." Extend to thousandths (0.156 = 1 tenth, 5 hundredths, 6 thousandths). Use a four-function calculator to count using decimals.

2 tenths
+ 3 hundredths
= 0.23

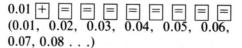

0.01 [+] [=] [=] [=] [=] [=] [=] [=] [=]
(0.01, 0.02, 0.03, 0.04, 0.05, 0.06, 0.07, 0.08 . . .)

Have students counting by 1's to 100 race with students counting by hundredths to 1 on a calculator.

8. Equivalence, comparison, and estimation

Use base-ten blocks. "Why is 0.23 equal to 23 hundredths?" (Each tenth is 10 hundredths.) "Why is 0.3 equal to 0.300?" (Each tenth is 100 thousandths.) "Why is 0.2 greater than 0.17?" (Two-tenths is more than one-tenth.) "Write decimals close to zero, close to one-half, and close to one."

For halves through fifths, develop important equivalents for fractions and decimals. Estimate computations (15 − 6.2 is about 9; 4.72 × 5.2 is about 25).

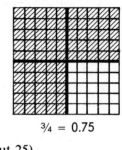

3/4 = 0.75

9. Computation—decimals

Use models and practical problems to develop each algorithm. Discuss rules that are similar and different for decimals and whole numbers. Use the calculator for all complicated decimal computations.

Reference

National Council of Teachers of Mathematics, Commission on Standards for School Mathematics. *Curriculum and Evaluation Standards for School Mathematics.* Reston, Va.: The Council, 1989. ◆

Space and Dimension

Geometry through the *Standards*

An underlying view of mathematics education expressed in the *Curriculum and Evaluation Standards* (NCTM 1989) is that a student should be actively involved both mentally and physically in constructing his or her own mathematical knowledge: "The K–4 curriculum should actively involve children in doing mathematics. . . . [They should] explore, justify, represent, solve, construct, discuss, use, investigate, describe, develop, and predict" (NCTM 1989, 17).

"Students [in grades 5–8] discover relationships . . . by constructing, drawing, measuring, visualizing, comparing, transforming, and classifying" (NCTM 1989, 112).

Geometry is exceptionally rich in opportunities for students to be involved in these ways. It also affords numerous occasions for teachers to address the four all-pervasive standards of problem solving, communication, reasoning, and connections. This article extends the ideas presented in "Implementing the *Standards*: The Geometry Standards in K–8 Mathematics" (Rowan 1990) and emphasizes a variety of ways to incorporate

Prepared by **Lorna J. Morrow**
University of Toronto
Toronto, ON M5S 2R7

Edited by **Thomas E. Rowan**
Montgomery County Public Schools
Rockville, MD 20850

The Editorial Panel welcomes readers' responses to this article or to any aspect of the Curriculum and Evaluation Standards for consideration for publication as an article or as a letter in "Readers' Dialogue."

FIGURE 1

An apparently simple geoboard problem

Find all possible noncongruent quadrilaterals that can be made on a 3 × 3 peg geoboard. For example:

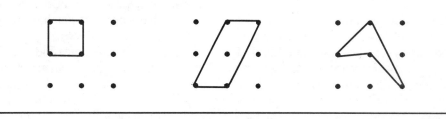

FIGURE 2

Students communicate geometric ideas.

"This has five sides, not four."

"These are the same but are turned different ways."

---

the recommendations in the curriculum standards into the elementary school geometry curriculum.

Geometry as Problem Solving

An apparently simple geoboard problem (**fig. 1**) can incorporate several suggestions from the curriculum standards on problem solving: "Students need to work on problems that may take hours . . . to solve. Although some may be relatively simple . . . others should involve small groups or an entire class working cooperatively" (NCTM 1989, 6).

When the problem is presented to stu-

dents in grades 3 to 5, students frequently begin working alone but soon share possibilities as they recognize that the problem will not be solved quickly and that a group effort is more likely to lead to a full solution.

As students *explore* the problem, they begin to *predict* the possible number of quadrilaterals (16). They *compare* figures with each other and *visualize* flips or turns needed to identify and eliminate congruent figures in different orientations. With a piece of tracing paper, they can physically compare the figures and *justify* the inclusion or deletion of one of the figures thus compared. As they share solutions, they identify duplicates in another's work and are often faced with

FIGURE 3

Outline a 4 × 4 geoboard on a 5 × 5 geoboard.

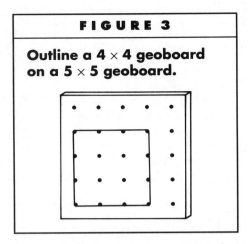

FIGURE 4

Try the same problems on a triangle or circle geoboard.

A triangle board   A circle board

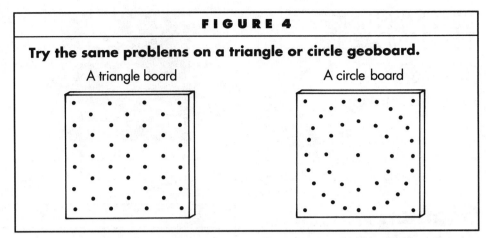

FIGURE 5

Simple problems permit the exploration of attributes by primary-level pupils.

On your geoboard, make a triangle with four pegs on the boundary.

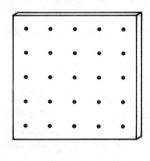

FIGURE 6

A problem can have more than one solution.

Some possible ways to make a triangle with four pegs on the boundary and one peg in the interior

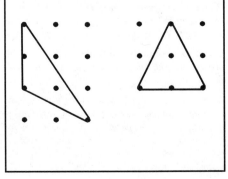

the task of *communicating* to that student just why a figure is inadmissable (see **fig. 2**).

The same problem used at a higher grade level can be extended by asking students to sort the quadrilaterals. The criteria chosen by the students might include parallel sides, congruent sides, congruent angles, symmetries, convex or concave properties, or area. "In internalizing the concept of a rectangle, a pupil needs a visual understanding of the figure. For example, a pupil learns to recognize rectangles and to differentiate them from other figures" (Del Grande 1990, 19).

Adjusting attributes within the original problem leads to problem posing, another important skill that students should be developing. "For all students to be mathematically literate, the instructional strategies must include collaborative experiences, . . . exploration activities that enable students to hypothesize and test, applications of mathematics, and experience in problem posing and writing" (Frye 1989, 7).

For example, instead of quadrilaterals, students may decide to investigate all possible noncongruent triangles (8 are possible), use a 4 × 4 instead of 3 × 3 peg geoboard (**fig. 3**), or use a triangle or circle geoboard instead of a square one (**fig. 4**).

Once students have learned to identify the attributes of a given problem, they can pose their own problems. Even primary-level students can explore the attributes of simple problems (**fig. 5**). Three attributes can be identified in the foregoing problems— the type of geoboard used, the number of sides in the polygon formed, and the number of pegs on the boundary. A fourth attribute can be added— the number of pegs in the interior of the figure.

Observing various solutions shows students that a problem can have more than one answer (see **fig. 6**).

Sorting out the attributes and dealing with one at a time gives students experience with a basic problem-solving strategy—make a simpler problem. It may also lead to an identification of irrelevant data. One group of second- and third-grade students began to include the number of pegs outside the figure in their problems but quickly realized that if they knew, for example, that six pegs appeared on the boundary and three pegs in the interior, then the number outside the figure must be 25 − 6 − 3, or 16.

Posing their own problems may lead students to problems with no solutions, for example, a triangle with five pegs on the boundary and two pegs inside. Although this problem is impossible on a standard geoboard, one second grader flipped his geoboard over to the circle side and solved the problem. He was learning not to be confined by assumed conditions in a problem.

As students investigate possible solutions to problems like these, they are gaining experience with basic polygons in various orientations. This experience helps students come to a better understanding of the nature of particular figures, for example, triangles. Students who have almost always seen triangles in the "standard" orientation,

often fail to recognize that the following figures are triangles (Rowan 1990, 25;

Thompson 1989, 26):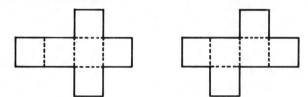

Geometry and Visualization

The ability to visualize figures and mentally "manipulate" them is a basic skill in mathematics. "Constructing new relationships and solving nonroutine problems are situations in which imagery is particularly valuable" (Wheatley 1990, 11).

Consider the value of giving a student a small hand mirror and asking him or her to walk backward across the classroom using the mirror image as a guide. Truck drivers spend weeks in training to develop this skill, and those of us who drive use it at least occasionally.

Dressmakers lay out pattern pieces to best advantage by rotating them to make the most economical use of the material and may flip pieces to cut both a left and a right side of a garment. This same skill can be developed with tangrams (Dunkels 1990; Jamski 1989; Silverman 1990), other space-filling activities, or even jigsaw puzzles.

Another spatial ability involves visualizing three-dimensional figures from two-dimensional drawings. Architects, builders, and car designers use this skill regularly. **Figure 7** gives two problems of this type.

Each of these problems can be extended further.

> A cube has eleven different nets. Try to find them all. Prove that your net makes a cube by cutting it out and folding it.

Students are eager to experiment to test their predictions (Mumme 1990, 20).

Shadows cast by three-dimensional figures help students see relationships between two-dimensional and three-dimensional figures. Extend this exercise by having students identify other figures that cast "square shadows" or build models that cast square shadows. Look for triangular shadows instead. How many shadows of different shapes can you produce with a cube? Use linking cubes to build three different figures that give square shadows. Once again, students should be encouraged to prove their answers through experimentation.

For other problems in visualization see

FIGURE 7

Two problems involving visualizing three-dimensional figures from two-dimensional drawings

1. Two nets of a cube are shown. Find at least two others.

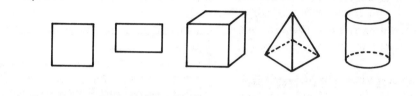

2. Which of the following figures could cast a shadow that is shaped like a square?

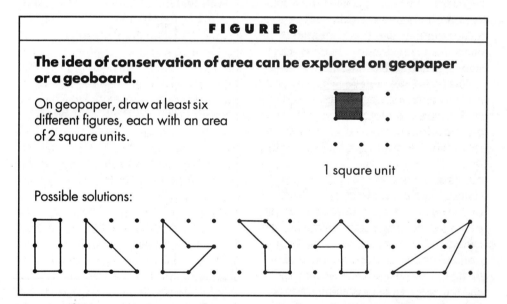

FIGURE 8

The idea of conservation of area can be explored on geopaper or a geoboard.

On geopaper, draw at least six different figures, each with an area of 2 square units.

1 square unit

Possible solutions:

Izard (1990), Owens (1990), and Sgroi (1990).

Geometry and Measurement

Tangram activities reinforce the idea of conservation of area. Not only young pupils find it difficult to accept the fact that a square and a triangle can have the same area (Robinson 1976, 21). A geoboard or geopaper problem can be used to explore this idea (see **fig. 8**). Students may wish to cut each figure apart and rearrange the pieces to form the 1×2 rectangle to verify their solutions.

Pentominoes, with "areas" of five squares, can be used in enjoyable and

worthwhile activities linking visualization and measurement (see, e.g., Onslow [1990]; Campbell and Bamberger [1990, 17]).

Older students can explore the Pythagorean relationship using triangles on geopaper (**fig. 9**). Drawing the triangles on geopaper allows students to investigate quickly and accurately the squares on the sides of several triangles. This investigation, in turn, allows them to draw conclusions and to make generalizations on the basis of several examples rather than just the two or three that traditionally appear in textbooks. Nonright triangles can also be explored to determine if the property holds. Students should be encouraged to "ponder such questions as,

Could it be another way? What would happen if . . . ?" (NCTM 1989, 113).

What would happen if we used isosceles triangles instead of right triangles? What if we drew semicircles on the sides instead of squares? What if we drew equilateral triangles (or other regular polygons) instead of squares?

Students can explore these and their own conjectures. The use of Logo or such computer programs as Geometric Supposer in conjunction with these activities furnishes a particularly rich experience and enhances students' understandings. See Del Grande and Morrow (forthcoming) and Geddes (1992) for suggested activities.

Geometry and Number

"[Children's] spatial capabilities frequently exceed their numerical skills, and tapping these strengths can foster an interest in mathematics and improve number understandings and skills" (NCTM 1989, 48).

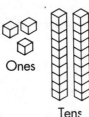

The use of base-ten blocks in the primary grades takes advantage of a child's intuitive feeling for shape and space. The blocks give pupils a visual representation of the relative sizes of various numbers. Simple patterns of building materials (**fig. 10**) can lead to first encounters with multiplication. The models built by the students furnish both visual and tactile experiences to assist in understanding. See also Newman and Turkel (1989) for an activity relating geometric and multiplication patterns through points on a circle.

Multiplication arrays are commonly used in middle elementary grades. They have remained a favorite for many years because they give students a good visual model. See Bruni and Silverman (1976) for related activities. These models can also be used to identify prime and square numbers (see **fig. 11**). Students quickly see that some numbers (i.e., primes) can be represented by only two rectangles; others (i.e., square num-

bers) by an odd number of rectangles, one of which is a square; and the number "1" by only one rectangle, making it unique.

Geometry and Connections

Since our world is geometric, readers should not be surprised that geometry can be a starting point for a multicultural study or for topics in science, geography, and visual arts.

Regular readers of the *Arithmetic Teacher* will remember articles by Zaslavsky (1989, 1991) and Taylor et al. (1991) in which examples of house structure, symmetry, and networks from African and American Indian cultures have been discussed.

Early American quilts are wonderful examples of pattern, symmetry, tessellations, and even optical illusions (Fisher 1990; Zaslavsky 1990). Crystal structure is closely related to symmetry in three-dimensional figures. A study of rocks and minerals can thus include a geometry component. Maps and topology can be used to explore the four-color theorem.

Such artists as Klee, Kandinsky, and Miro often painted entirely with geometric forms. Students can explore art books to find examples of geometry. They can create their own works of art along similar lines. Escher explored transformations of basic figures to produce exotic tessellations that motivate students to create their own (Giganti and Cittadino 1990).

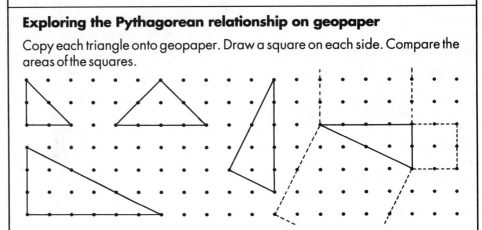

FIGURE 9

Exploring the Pythagorean relationship on geopaper

Copy each triangle onto geopaper. Draw a square on each side. Compare the areas of the squares.

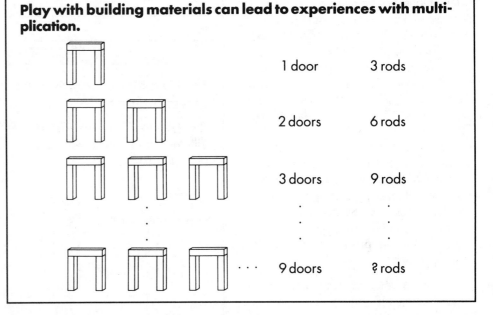

FIGURE 10

Play with building materials can lead to experiences with multiplication.

	1 door	3 rods
	2 doors	6 rods
	3 doors	9 rods
	9 doors	? rods

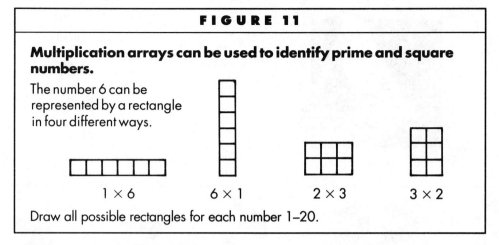

FIGURE 11

Multiplication arrays can be used to identify prime and square numbers.

The number 6 can be represented by a rectangle in four different ways.

1×6 6×1 2×3 3×2

Draw all possible rectangles for each number 1–20.

The collection of slides published by NCTM gives many more examples of, and suggestions for, exploring geometry in nature, art, and architecture (Engelhardt 1987). "Exercises that ask children to visualize . . . will help develop their spatial sense . . . [which is] necessary for interpreting, understanding, and appreciating our inherently geometric world" (NCTM 1989, 48).

Geometry as a Pervasive Standard

The first four standards (Problem Solving, Communication, Reasoning, Connections) have been identified as pervasive—as underlying the whole curriculum rather than being topics unto themselves.

An exploration of geometry and geometric topics suggests that this standard too is, in many ways, a foundation for, or a connection among, many other topics in mathematics, in other areas of the curriculum, and in real life.

Spatial ability has been identified by Gardner (1984) as one of the seven intelligences of the human mind. Spatial abilities can be improved through a good geometry program (Del Grande 1986). Such a program goes a long way toward meeting the goals articulated recently by Frye (1989, 6):

Making it possible for every student to achieve mathematical power is indeed worth the effort. This power is the ability to explore, conjecture, and reason logically as well as use a variety of mathematical methods to solve nonroutine problems effectively. It is achieved not by doing just pencil-and-paper practice but through a variety of teaching and learning methods that enable students to progress successfully.

Forty-six years ago, Sifton (1945, 1) expressed a similar view in the Eighteenth Yearbook: "We know . . . that for *our* pupils, learning *must* be something more than seeing and hearing; for them mathematics *must* be a means for *doing* things."

Geometry, with its wealth of applications and its ease of application of manipulatives, is an important part of the K–8 curriculum and will help us approach this ideal of mathematics education.

Bibliography

Brown, Stephen I., and Marion I. Walter. "The Art of Problem Posing." Hillsdale, N.J.: Lawrence Erlbaum Associates, 1983.

Bruni, James V. "Problem Solving for the Primary Grades." *Arithmetic Teacher* 29 (February 1982):10–15.

Bruni, James V., and Helene J. Silverman. "Let's Do It: The Multiplication Facts: Once More, with Understanding." *Arithmetic Teacher* 23 (October 1976):402–9.

Burger, William F. "One Point of View: An Active Approach to Geometry." *Arithmetic Teacher* 36 (November 1988):2.

Campbell, Patricia F., and Honi J. Bamberger. "The Vision of Problem Solving in the *Standards*." *Arithmetic Teacher* 37 (May 1990): 14–17.

Del Grande, John J. "Can Children's Spatial Perception Be Improved by Inserting a Transformation Geometry Component into their Mathematics Program?" Ph.D. diss., University of Toronto, 1986.

———. "Spatial Sense." *Arithmetic Teacher* 37 (February 1990):14–20.

Del Grande, John, and Lorna Morrow. *Geometry and Spatial Sense. Curriculum and Evaluation Standards for School Mathematics* Addenda Series, Grades K–6, edited by Miriam A. Leiva. Reston, Va.: National Council of Teachers of Mathematics, forthcoming.

Dunkels, Andrejs. "Making and Exploring Tangrams." *Arithmetic Teacher* 37 (February 1990):38–42.

Engelhardt, John, comp. *Geometry in Our World.* Slides and commentary compiled by John Engelhardt. Reston, Va.: National Council of Teachers of Mathematics, 1987.

Fisher, Laura. *Quilts of Illusion.* New York: Sterling Publishing Co., 1990.

Frye, Shirley M. "The NCTM *Standards*— Challenges for All Classrooms." *Arithmetic Teacher* 36 (May 1989):4–7.

Gardner, Howard. "The Seven Frames of Mind." *Psychology Today*, June 1984, 21–26.

Geddes, Dorothy. *Geometry in the Middle Grades. Curriculum and Evaluation Standards for School Mathematics* Addenda Series, Grades 5–8, edited by Frances R. Curcio. Reston, Va.: National Council of Teachers of Mathematics, 1992.

Giganti, Paul, Jr., and Mary Jo Cittadino. "The Art of Tessellation." *Arithmetic Teacher* 37 (March 1990):6–16.

Izard, John. "Developing Spatial Skills with Three-Dimensional Puzzles." *Arithmetic Teacher* 37 (February 1990):44–47.

Jamski, William D. "Six Hard Pieces." *Arithmetic Teacher* 37 (October 1989):34–35.

Moses, Barbara. "Developing Spatial Thinking in the Middle Grades: Designing a Space Station." *Arithmetic Teacher* 37 (February 1990):59–63.

Mumme, Judith, and Nancy Shepherd. "Implementing the *Standards*: Communication in Mathematics." *Arithmetic Teacher* 38 (September 1990):18–22.

National Council of Teachers of Mathematics, Commission on Standards for School Mathematics. *Curriculum and Evaluation Standards for School Mathematics*. Reston, Va.: The Council, 1989.

Newman, Claire M., and Susan B. Turkel. "Integrating Arithmetic and Geometry with Numbered Points on a Circle." *Arithmetic Teacher* 36 (January 1989):28–30.

Onslow, Barry. "Pentominoes Revisited." *Arithmetic Teacher* 37 (May 1990):5–9.

Owens, Douglas T. "Research into Practice: Spatial Abilities." *Arithmetic Teacher* 37 (February 1990):48–51.

Robinson, Edith. "Mathematical Foundations of the Development of Spatial and Geometrical Concepts." *In Space and Geometry: Papers from a Research Workshop*, 7–27. Columbus, Ohio: ERIC, 1976.

Rowan, Thomas E. "Implementing the *Standards*: The Geometry Standards in K–8 Mathematics." *Arithmetic Teacher* 37 (February 1990):24–28.

Sgroi, Richard J. "Communicating about Spatial Relationships." *Arithmetic Teacher* 37 (February 1990):21–23.

Sifton, Edith. "Multi-Sensory Aids: Some Theory and a Few Practices." *In Multi-Sensory Aids in the Teaching of Mathematics*, Eighteenth Yearbook of the National Council of Teachers of Mathematics, compiled by the Committee on Multi-Sensory Aids of the National Council of Teachers of Mathematics, 1–15. New York: Bureau of Publications, Teachers College, Columbia University, 1945.

———. "IDEAS." *Arithmetic Teacher* 37 (February 1990):29–37.

Taylor, Lyn, Ellen Stevens, John J. Peregoy, and Barbara Bath. "American Indians, Mathematical Attitudes, and the *Standards*." *Arithmetic Teacher* 38 (February 1991):14–21.

Thompson, Alba G. "Implementing the Standards: Assessing Students' Learning to Inform Teaching: The Message in NCTM's Evaluation Standards." *Arithmetic Teacher* 37 (December 1989):22–26.

Wheatley, Grayson H. "One Point of View: Spatial Sense and Mathematics Learning." *Arithmetic Teacher* 37 (February 1990):10–11.

Zaslavsky, Claudia. "Multicultural Mathematics Education for Middle Grades." *Arithmetic Teacher* 38 (February 1991):8–13.

———. "People Who Live in Round Houses." *Arithmetic Teacher* 37 (September 1989):18–21.

———. "Symmetry in American Folk Art." *Arithmetic Teacher* 38 (September 1990):6–12. ◆

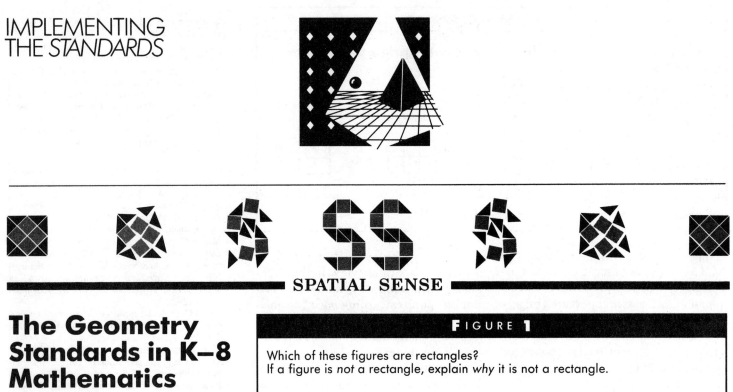

SPATIAL SENSE

The Geometry Standards in K–8 Mathematics

A group of fifth graders was observed doing a textbook exercise in which they were to identify which of a set of five geometric shapes were rectangles (**fig. 1**). Their efforts were interesting and illustrated the concerns that some mathematics educators have about our current teaching of geometry. It was obvious that most of the students thought they knew what a rectangle was. But even those who exhibited this confidence had difficulty identifying the proper figures and explaining to their classmates why a trapezoid is not a rectangle or that the sides of a rectangle do not have to be horizontal or vertical, as in shape C in **figure 1**. They seemed to have an incomplete knowledge of this geometric shape, which is usually introduced in kindergarten or first grade.

Geometry inspires a wide variety of opinions whenever mathematics teachers discuss the curriculum. It doesn't seem to matter whether those in the discussion are elementary school, middle school, or high school mathe-

Edited and prepared by **Thomas E. Rowan**
Montgomery County Public Schools
Rockville, MD 20850

The Editorial Panel welcomes readers' responses to this article or to any aspect of the Standards.

F IGURE 1

Which of these figures are rectangles?
If a figure is *not* a rectangle, explain *why* it is not a rectangle.

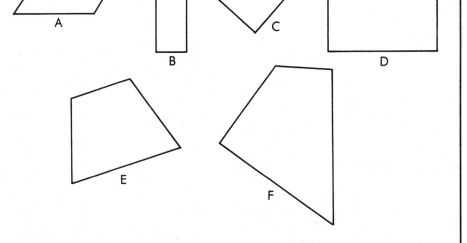

---

matics teachers. Most agree that geometric knowledge and concepts are important for students to acquire. When, how, and what knowledge should be acquired are not so well agreed on, however. Research by the van Hieles of Holland, which has been replicated and extended by some American researchers, has elicited various recommendations with respect to these questions (Crowley 1987).

The *Curriculum and Evaluation*

Standards for School Mathematics (*Standards*) (NCTM 1989) includes geometry and spatial sense for grades K–4 and 5–8 (**fig. 2**). It affirms the importance of studying these topics and proposes approaches that address the findings of recent research, as well as the developmental levels of students in these grades. Students in grades K–8 need to meet geometric ideas initially through first-hand experiences with the geometric nature of the world in which they live. Vocabulary, which has played such a prominent role in these grades in earlier programs, must grow out of experience and understanding. Of course the abilities to name geometric shapes, such as rectangles, and to apply geometric relationships, such as that the sum of the measures of the angles of a triangle is 180 degrees, are useful. But the verbalization of these names and relationships should grow out of experience that leads to the development of underlying concepts.

The fifth-grade students who knew the word *rectangle* but could not sort rectangles from sets with other quadrilaterals, even though they could name a rectangle when that was the only shape presented, probably needed to have experienced more activities in which they first worked with whole shapes, then analyzed the characteristics of those shapes, and then observed the relationships among those shapes. To understand the concept of a rectangle, they needed to have had opportunities to recognize rectangular shapes as a whole in various orientations, then to identify specific characteristics of a rectangle (e.g., sides, angles), then to compare it to other shapes to consider similarities and differences.

Settings in which students have opportunities to explore, invent, and discuss in their own words may be the most productive for helping students attain a firm foundation in geometry. Teacher wait time, early acceptance of students' language, and cooperative groups that offer greater opportunities for all students to verbalize their ideas may be critical components in the formula for successful teaching of geometry.

Activities for Grades K–4

The *Standards* calls for students to investigate two- and three-dimensional geometry. Students need to become familiar with the characteristics of many kinds of solid and plane figures, such as *spheres*, *cones*, *rectangular solids*, and *rectangles*, *triangles*, and *circles*. It is vital at all grade levels, but especially in grades K–2, that vocabulary such as this be developed

---

FIGURE 2

Geometry and Spatial-Sense Standards for K–4 and 5–8

K–4 Standard 9
In grades K–4, the mathematics curriculum should include two- and three-dimensional geometry so that students can—
- describe, model, draw, and classify shapes;
- investigate and predict the results of combining, subdividing, and changing shapes;
- develop spatial sense;
- relate geometric ideas to number and measurement ideas;
- recognize and appreciate geometry in their world.

5–8 Standard 12
In grades 5–8, the mathematics curriculum should include the study of the geometry of one, two, and three dimensions in a variety of situations so that students can—
- identify, describe, compare, and classify geometric figures;
- visualize and represent geometric figures with special attention to developing spatial sense;
- explore transformations of geometric figures;
- represent and solve problems using geometric models;
- understand and apply geometric properties and relationships;
- develop an appreciation of geometry as a means of describing the physical world.

From Curriculum and Evaluation Standards for School Mathematics (NCTM 1989)

---

through activities that call forth the words naturally.

In kindergarten and first grade, pupils should be given many opportunities to find shapes that match other shapes. This matching can be done through games that resemble scavenger hunts, in which pupils move in pairs through their classroom, or perhaps the school building, locating shapes that match a shape or shapes that have been assigned to them. When they find a shape that matches, they stick on it a paper model of their assigned shape. They are encouraged to discuss their decisions in their assigned pairs and to share their discussions with the class, describing what clues helped them decide a figure was or was not a rectangle, circle, triangle, cone, sphere, cylinder, and so on. They need to relate pictures of three-dimensional objects with an actual object and to discover how a plane, or "flat," figure like a rectangle or a circle appears as the perimeter of a "face" of a solid figure.

A related activity involves having pupils create a "shapes mural": Give pairs of pupils sets of paper models of areas of geometric shapes—various kinds of triangles, squares, rectangles

that are not squares, circles, ovals that are not circles, and other unfamiliar shapes. Help them work together to contribute to a class "shapes mural," which might show a scene with animals, trees, and houses or use some other theme. After several weeks, revisit the mural and give the pupils another set of paper shapes, including shapes like the ones used to make the mural. Have them try to locate the various shapes in the mural and name any of the shapes they know. Also have them identify or describe any of the new shapes that do not appear in the mural at all. This activity involves pupils in identifying congruent shapes in various positions or orientations on the mural. Using shapes that are similar (same shape but not necessarily the same size) offers rich opportunities for further exploration of relationships among shapes.

Young children also enjoy cutting apart shapes and trying to reassemble them from pieces **(fig. 3)** or creating their own shapes (see Dunkels in this issue). Tangramlike investigations are excellent for visualizing and predicting the results of subdividing and combining parts of plane regions in

FIGURE 3

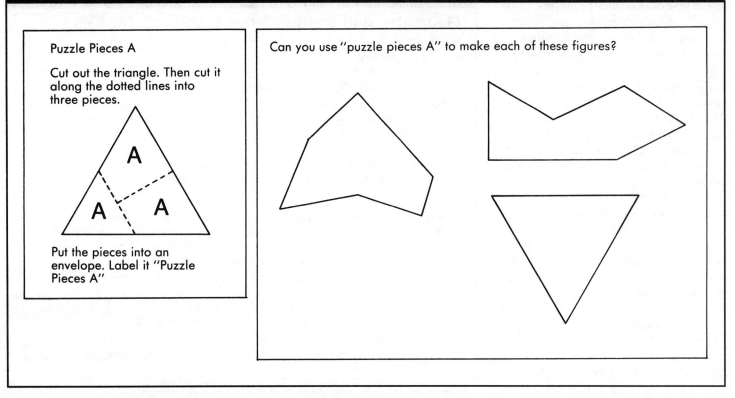

Puzzle Pieces A

Cut out the triangle. Then cut it along the dotted lines into three pieces.

Put the pieces into an envelope. Label it "Puzzle Pieces A"

Can you use "puzzle pieces A" to make each of these figures?

FIGURE 4

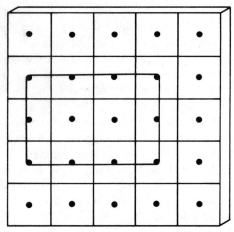

On the geoboard make a shape that has four sides and square corners. Draw that shape on your dot paper.

On your geoboard make as many *different* shapes as you can that have four sides and square corners. Copy each one onto dot paper. How are they different?

On your geoboard can you change a four-sided shape with square corners into a four-sided shape *without* square corners? Try it. Copy the shape you make onto dot paper.

Geoboard dot paper

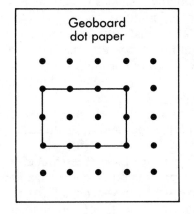

different ways. An important component of these activities is the discussion. When pupils complete a puzzle, ask them to tell their partners, group, or the class what clues they used to help decide how the shape should be reassembled. ("I knew it had to have three corners, but if I had put it that way it would have had four.")

Geoboards are especially valuable because they allow students to create plane figures easily and to transform them in different ways. Once made with elastic bands on a geoboard, the figures can be recorded on geoboard dot paper. Drawing these models of geometric figures on dot paper helps students focus on the specific characteristics of different shapes **(fig. 4)**.

After having experience creating shapes on a geoboard, students can be helped by an activity like the following to describe the characteristics, location, and position of shapes: Have students work in pairs. Partners sit back to back, with one student making a shape on the geoboard, or on geoboard dot paper, without the other seeing the shape. That person then describes the shape clearly enough so that his or her partner can re-create it on his or her geoboard. A third stu-

Cover the owl shape with pattern blocks.

How many *different* ways can you do it?

Keep a record of the ways you used.

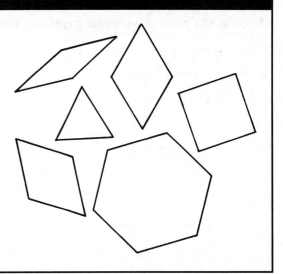

dent can also be used to observe the two players from a point where both the original shape and the re-creation can be seen. The observer gives clues as to successful communication (such as "yes" or "no," "you're getting hot" or "cold," etc.). Making shapes on a geoboard facilitates the correction of errant tries.

Pattern blocks are also useful for visualizing how shapes can be combined to form other shapes and for investigating relationships of the sides and angles of shapes. **Figure 5** offers some examples of these investigations.

Activities for Grades 5–8

In grades 5–8 the types of activities begun in the lower grades can be extended, and new levels of sophistication can be added. For example, describing a created or given shape for another student to re-create without seeing the original can be extended to more complex shapes or into three dimensions (e.g., using wooden or plastic cubes to make models of geometric structures for others to re-create). Similarly, more complex tangramlike activities are valuable for visualizing alternative ways to form a shape and how shapes look in different positions.

At the upper grade levels, students can more easily make models of three-dimensional geometric figures and ex-

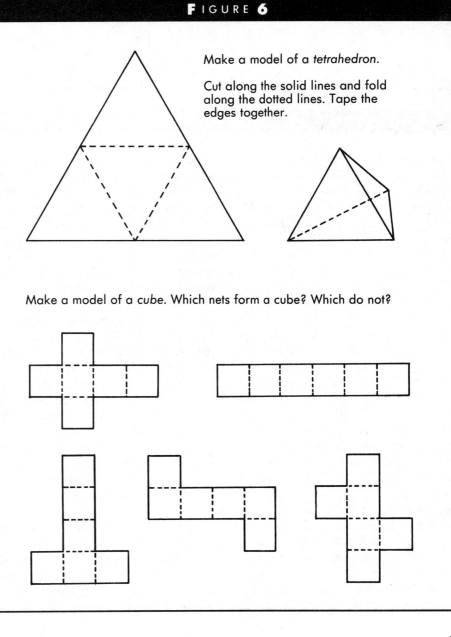

Make a model of a *tetrahedron*.

Cut along the solid lines and fold along the dotted lines. Tape the edges together.

Make a model of a *cube*. Which nets form a cube? Which do not?

FIGURE 7

Students can discover basic area formulas.

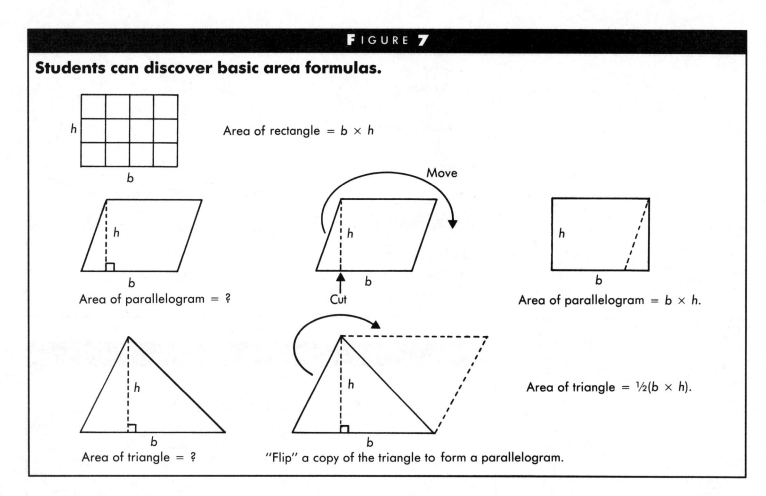

Area of rectangle = $b \times h$

Area of parallelogram = ?

Move

Cut

Area of parallelogram = $b \times h$.

Area of triangle = $\frac{1}{2}(b \times h)$.

Area of triangle = ?

"Flip" a copy of the triangle to form a parallelogram.

plore the various nets used to create those models (**fig. 6**). They can also explore orthogonal projections of a figure and how a figure looks from different perspectives (see Izard in this issue).

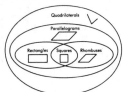

After many experiences in describing and comparing the properties of such shapes as quadrilaterals, students at this level can begin to organize information about these shapes by participating in the development of a diagram that shows the interrelationships of various quadrilaterals. In this way they begin to see the parallelogram as a special type of quadrilateral, rectangles and rhombuses as special types of parallelograms, and a square as having properties of both the rhombus and the rectangle.

Through guided-discovery activities, students can see additional characteristics of shapes and relationships among shapes. For example, students can cut the corners off a variety of

paper models of triangles and explore what happens when those angles are combined to form one angle, leading to the "discovery" of the sum-of-the-angles relationship, which exists in all triangles. The same kind of discovery activity can lead students to see that two triangles can sometimes be put together to form a quadrilateral. If the triangles have one congruent or matching side, a quadrilateral can be formed. When the two triangles are congruent, parallelograms or other shapes can be formed. Similarly, they can explore various ways that more than two triangles might be combined

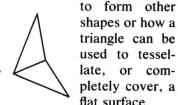

to form other shapes or how a triangle can be used to tessellate, or completely cover, a flat surface.

By exploring shapes and transforming models of shapes, students can discover basic area formulas. **Figure 7** illustrates the development of formulas for the areas of the parallelogram and the triangle, starting with the ba-

sic formula for the area of a rectangle.

Geometric exploration can be used to develop a better concept of area and perimeter. Can the student construct a polygon with a perimeter of 20 units inside a polygon with a perimeter of 15 units? Why or why not? Can the student construct a polygon with an area of 20 square units inside a polygon with an area of 15 square units? Why or why not?

In conclusion, geometry has much to offer for the mathematical development of our students. Teaching geometry so that it is meaningful to our students is important. The ideas of the *Standards* are designed to help us do that.

References

Crowley, Mary L. "The van Hiele Model of the Development of Geometric Thought." In *Learning and Teaching Geometry, K–12,* 1987 Yearbook of the National Council of Teachers of Mathematics, edited by Mary Montgomery Lindquist and Albert P. Shulte. Reston, Va.: The Council, 1987.

National Council of Teachers of Mathematics, Commission on Standards for School Mathematics. *Curriculum and Evaluation Standards for School Mathematics.* Reston, Va.: The Council, 1989. ♣

The Measurement Standards

Clear expectations for the measurement curricula of grades K–8 are expressed in the *Curriculum and Evaluation Standards for School Mathematics* (NCTM 1989). The statements in **figure 1** are discussed in the *Standards*. Central to both the K–4 and 5–8 standards is the process of measuring, which can help students build understanding about measuring and make connections among various measurement concepts and skills.

The process of measuring is the same for every measurable attribute: an appropriate unit is chosen, that unit is compared to the object being measured, and the number of units is reported. Let us consider the process of measuring using the little finger as an example. After deciding to measure the length of the finger, we need to decide on an appropriate unit—a unit whose nature and size is determined by the attribute to be measured and by the degree of accuracy desired. It would not be expedient to choose a liter (a unit of capacity) or a mile (a unit of length that is too large). Suppose we choose a centimeter as the unit. We then compare the centimeter with our finger. If we had con-

Edited by **Thomas E. Rowan**
Montgomery County Public Schools
Rockville, MD 20850

Prepared by **Mary Montgomery Lindquist**
Columbus College
Columbus, GA 31907

The Editorial Panel welcomes readers' reactions to this article or to any aspect of the Standards.

FIGURE 1

Measurement standards for K–4 and 5–8

K–4 Standard 10

In grades K–4, the mathematics curriculum should include measurement so that students can—
• understand the attributes of length, capacity, weight, area, volume, time, temperature, and angle;
• develop the process of measuring and concepts related to units of measurement;
• make and use estimates of measurement;
• make and use measurements in problem and everyday situations.

5–8 Standard 13

In grades 5–8, the mathematics curriculum should include extensive concrete experiences using measurement so that students can—
• extend their understanding of the process of measurement;
• estimate, make, and use measurements to describe and compare phenomena;
• select appropriate units and tools to measure to the degree of accuracy required in a particular situation;
• understand the structure and use of systems of measurement;
• extend their understanding of the concepts of perimeter, area, volume, angle measure, capacity, and weight and mass;
• develop the concepts of rates and other derived and indirect measurements;
• develop formulas and procedures for determining measures to solve problems.

FIGURE 2

Pattern blocks from tallest to shortest

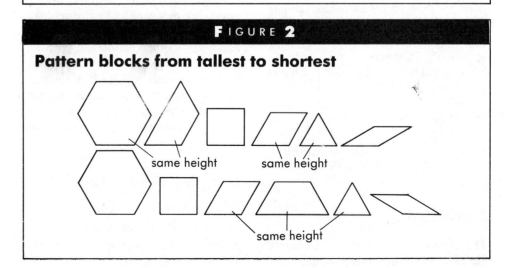

---

necting centimeter cubes, we could make a rod as long as our finger and count the number of centimeters. If we had a ruler, the units would be numbered and thus we would not have to count. Lastly, we report the number of units, say eight centimeters.

Students should think about this process for several reasons. They will discover the decisions to be made when measuring—what to measure, what unit to use, and how to compare the two (by counting, using an instrument, or using a formula). The numbers that result from measuring will have meaning, and the need to specify the unit will be clear. Students will see how measuring length is like, and also different from, measuring area and how measuring in grams is like measuring in ounces. In general, they will see differences and similarities in measuring different attributes, and they will learn that measuring an attribute involves the same process no matter which unit of measurement is chosen.

In analyzing performance on measurement items on the fourth mathematics assessment of the NAEP (Lindquist and Kouba 1989), I was struck with how well our students did if the item involved a measurement of length smaller than a textbook page or if the item was exactly like simple textbook problems and how poorly they did otherwise. Students should not be expected to learn about capacity, about feet, about meters, about weight, about surface area, about volume only from exercises on a page. They need to explore attributes and use measuring instruments. They need to explore relationships among figures to determine efficient ways to count the number of units rather than memorize formulas. They need to learn to make decisions about what is to be measured and how it will be measured. They need to experience being unable to measure an attribute with inappropriate units (e.g., measuring weight with units of capacity). That is, they need to use the measurement process.

Activities

The activities that follow emphasize the process of measuring using count-

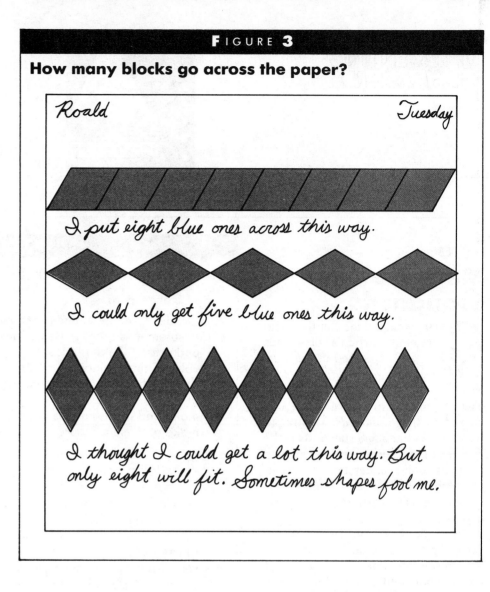

FIGURE 3

How many blocks go across the paper?

Roald   Tuesday

I put eight blue ones across this way.

I could only get five blue ones this way.

I thought I could get a lot this way. But only eight will fit. Sometimes shapes fool me.

ing to find the measurement. Activities of this type help students understand the attribute being measured and build a foundation for meaningful use of measuring instruments and formulas. All the activities use pattern blocks, but at the various grade levels different attributes (length, area, and angle) are measured. If pattern blocks are not available, the activities can be adapted to other geometric pieces. I have chosen pattern blocks because their use enables students to learn about geometry while learning about measuring. Some of the activities are also tied to other such topics as art, graphing, and writing.

Length (primary level)

Who is taller?

This activity affords experience with direct comparison of objects, a necessary prerequisite to comparing a unit

with a length. It also helps pupils see that any real object has many dimensions.

Give a small group of pupils one of each of the pattern blocks. Have them decide which of two blocks is taller by setting each piece on edge on a table. Have pupils compare the various dimensions of like pieces by turning one of them (often they will have to hold it so it touches the base but does not sit alone) to make it taller. Then have them put one of each block in order from tallest to shortest. Their answers could vary as shown in **figure 2** depending on which way they turn the block. They will find other solutions if they hold the piece upright rather than set it on an edge.

How many does it take?

This activity gives pupils the opportunity to line up units to measure a length. This idea is built on in the next

FIGURE 4

Two lengths of a hexagon

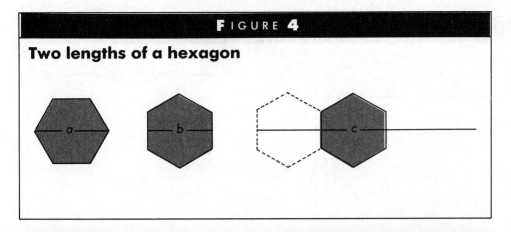

FIGURE 5

A graph for the length of an object

activity in which pupils explore measuring with different units. Each pupil needs blocks of one color and a sheet of paper. Ask pupils to make a line of the blocks as long as the width of the paper or across the paper. Have them outline the blocks to show how they placed them. Encourage pupils to try several ways and to tell about the various ways they find. (See **fig. 3**.)

How long?

In this activity the pupils learn that different units give different measures of the same length. This discovery depends on the pupils' understanding that each pattern piece has many different lengths. Discuss how to use each piece as a unit of measurement after deciding which length to use. For example, on the yellow hexagon pupils could choose length *a* or length *b*. For length *b*, the piece would be moved as shown in **figure 4**. Give each pair of pupils one of each of the blocks and have them measure the length of their mathematics book and then complete a graph like the one in **figure 5**. After the graphs are finished, discuss the various measurements. Why were more green blocks required than yellow? Why did Susy and Jim's answer differ from the answer Tony and Latisha got using the yellow block for the unit of measurement?

Area (intermediate level)

Equal areas

In this introductory activity, the students explore the area of the pattern blocks and develop an understanding of the area relationships among the pieces. Have each student make a shape with 2 red blocks and then

FIGURE 6

Equal areas

RED	BLUE	GREEN
2		
4		
6		
3		

FIGURE 7

Cover me.

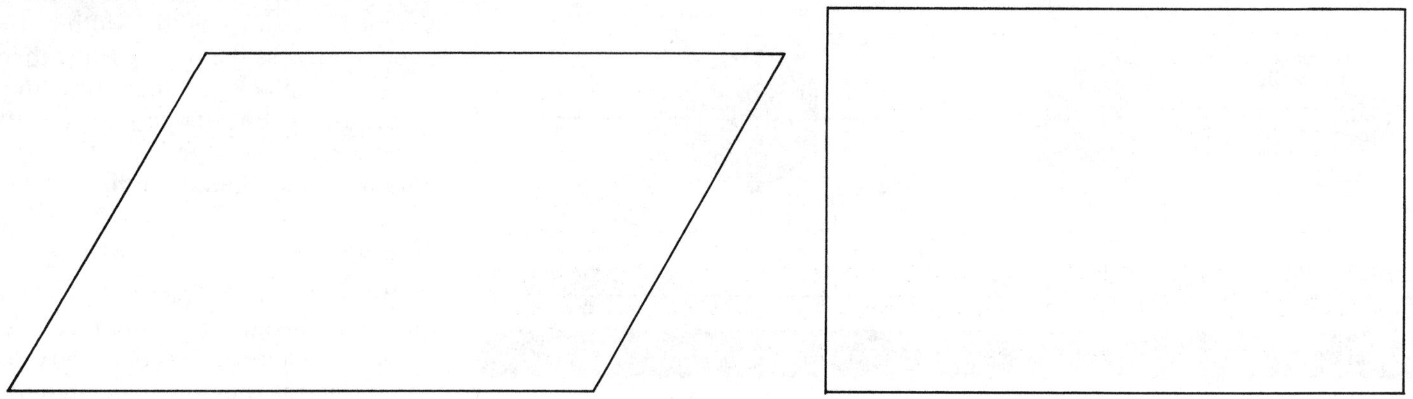

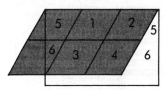

FIGURE 8

Coverings of the rectangle and parallelogram

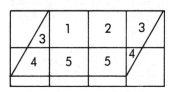

More than five orange blocks

More than six blue blocks

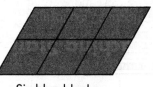

Six blue blocks

Six orange blocks

FIGURE 9

A floor tiling

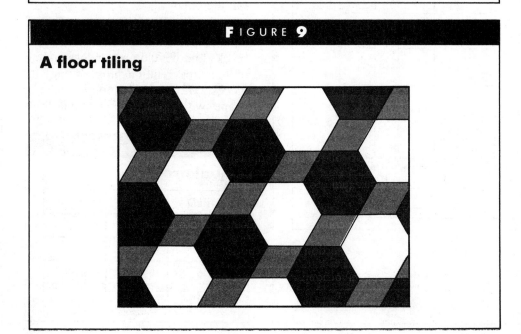

cover it first with blue blocks and then with green blocks to complete the chart in **figure 6** (the number of blocks may need to be stated as more than 4 but less than 5 or as about 4½). Extend their thinking to see if they can tell how many blue blocks would be required to cover a shape made from 20 red blocks, from 25 red blocks, from 16 green blocks, and from 100 green blocks.

Cover me

In this activity the students cover shapes and count the number of units to explore the need for using the same

FIGURE 10

How large is each angle?

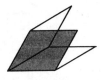

The small angle on the blue is 2 units.

The large angle on the red is 4 units.

FIGURE 11

The sum of the angles of a polygon

Number of sides of the polygon	3	4	5	6	7	8
Sum of the angles using the white unit	6					

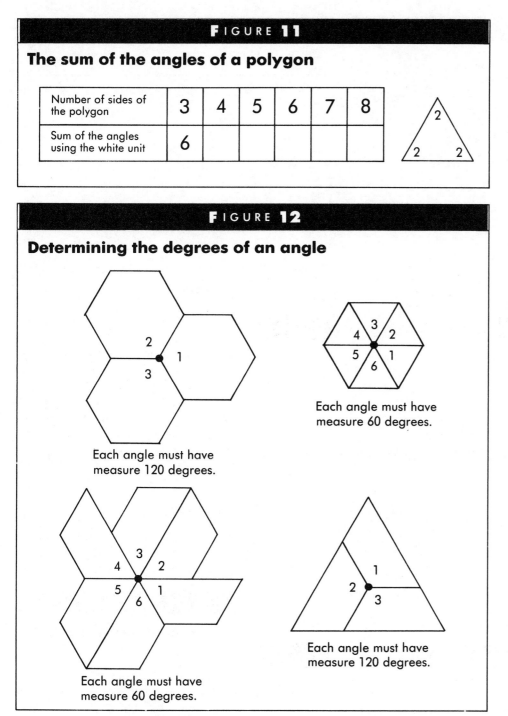

FIGURE 12

Determining the degrees of an angle

Each angle must have measure 120 degrees.

Each angle must have measure 60 degrees.

Each angle must have measure 60 degrees.

Each angle must have measure 120 degrees.

unit when comparing areas. Give each student a copy of the parallelogram and rectangle in **figure 7**. Ask which shape is larger in area. Let them cover each with pattern blocks to see if they can arrive at an answer. Help them to see that no unit is particularly useful for covering both and that they will need to do some estimating to arrive at an answer (see **fig. 8** for some possible coverings). If the students are not convinced, then they could cut up the parallelogram and see that it fits inside the rectangle. Follow up this

activity by having students make a shape from the pattern pieces and trace around its perimeter. Have them compare their shapes with those of other students to see if they can tell which is larger by overlaying other pattern pieces when necessary.

Design a tile floor

This activity illustrates a use of area in everyday life. The students design a floor of a six-foot-by-eight-foot room and determine how many blocks of

each kind are needed to complete the floor. Use a scale (a one-inch block equals one foot) or design a part of the floor at the actual size. Tiles may have to be cut to fit the edge of the room. (See **fig. 9** for one tiling.)

Angles (upper level)

How large is each angle?

This activity introduces measuring angles with an arbitrary or nonstandard unit. Again, it illustrates the measurement process: choose a unit, compare it to the object, and report the number of units.

Use the smaller angle on the white block as an arbitrary unit. Find the size of each of the other angles on the other blocks in relationship to this unit. See **figure 10** for a sample of the results of measuring other angles with this unit.

What is the sum of the angles?

Using an arbitrary unit of measure students discover that the sum of the angles of a polygon depends on the number of its sides. Use as the unit of measurement the smaller angle on the white piece. Fill in the chart in **figure 11**. Polygons with five, seven, and eight sides will need to be made by putting the blocks together.

How many degrees in each angle?

This activity makes the transition to measuring angles with degrees. Use the fact that there are 360 degrees around a point to figure out the size of each of the angles on the blocks by seeing how many blocks are required to fill the area around the point (always using the same angle of each block at the point) (see **fig. 12**). Relate this activity to the previous one and find the number of degrees in each of the polygons.

References

Lindquist, Mary M., and Vicky L. Kouba. "Measurement." In *Results from the Fourth Mathematics Assessment of the National Assessment of Educational Progress*, edited by Mary M. Lindquist, 35–43. Reston, Va.: The Council, 1989.

National Council of Teachers of Mathematics. Commission on Standards for School Mathematics. *Curriculum and Evaluation Standards for School Mathematics*. Reston, Va.: The Council, 1989. ▰

Data Collection and Interpretation

4

The Statistics Standards in K–8 Mathematics

"**I**s the rate of homelessness increasing?"

"Are we really protecting humpback whales?"

"Will recycling make a difference?"

Informed citizens in our society must be prepared to deal with complex issues such as these. We need to know how to question and interpret data that are presented to us and to make sense of graphs and charts used by newspapers and television to report data. The more comfortable our students become with understanding, manipulating, and interpreting information, the better prepared they will be for such responsibilities. To participate as informed citizens necessitates both comfort with, and flexible use of,

Prepared by **Susan N. Friel**
  and **Rebecca B. Corwin**

Edited by **Thomas E. Rowan**
Montgomery County Public Schools
Rockville, MD 20850

Susan Friel was coprincipal investigator on the Used Numbers Project. She currently is director of the Mathematics and Science Education Network at the University of North Carolina in Chapel Hill, NC 27599-3345. Rebecca Corwin was a lead author on the Used Numbers Project. She shares her time between the Technical Education Research Centers, Cambridge, Massachusetts, where she is a senior associate, and Lesley College, Cambridge, MA 02138, where she is professor of education.

The Editorial Panel welcomes readers' responses to this article or to any aspect of the Standards *for consideration for publication as an article or as a letter in "Readers' Dialogue."*

FIGURE 1

In grades K–4, the mathematics curriculum should include experiences with data analysis and probability so that students can—

♦ collect, organize, and describe data;

♦ construct, read, and interpret displays of data;

♦ formulate and solve problems that involve collecting and analyzing data;

♦ explore concepts of chance.

In grades 5–8, the mathematics curriculum should include exploration of statistics in real-world situations so that students can—

♦ systematically collect, organize, and describe data;

♦ construct, read, and interpret tables, charts, and graphs;

♦ make inferences and convincing arguments that are based on data analysis;

♦ evaluate arguments that are based on data analysis;

♦ develop an appreciation for statistical methods as powerful means for decision making.

Quoted from *Curriculum and Evaluation Standards for School Mathematics* by the National Council of Teachers of Mathematics, Commission on Standards for School Mathematics (Reston, Va.: The Council, 1989, 54, 105)

---

statistics—using numbers to describe, summarize, and interpret reality.

The National Council of Teachers of Mathematics's *Curriculum and Evaluation Standards for School Mathematics* (*Standards*) (1989) offers a vision of school mathematics that recognizes the importance of statistics and data analysis in the mathematics curriculum. Elementary and middle-grades curriculum recommendations include standards directed toward data analysis (see **fig. 1**). These standards supply the context for what we mean by statistics and how it should be implemented.

A knowledge of statistics and data analysis helps students answer questions, make decisions, and develop predictions using information. Learning statistics can be a vehicle to give meaning to computational skills that are too often isolated from relevant contexts.

Teaching Statistics

Collecting, exploring, and describing data are appropriate central themes for grades K–4. As students move into the fifth and sixth grades, emphasis shifts to making comparisons among and between different sets of data; more explicit attention is given to using measures of central tendency, particularly the median and

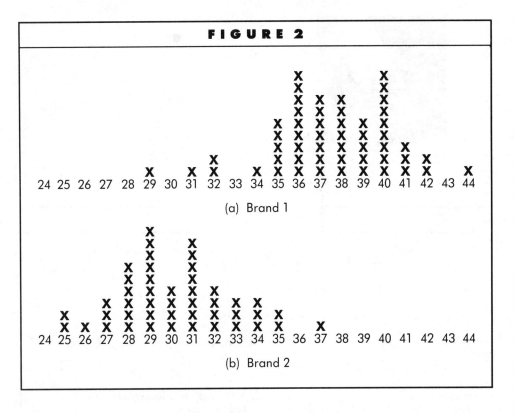

FIGURE 2

(a) Brand 1

(b) Brand 2

and can discuss the conditions for a sample to represent the population.

Primary Grades

Young pupils are fascinated with counting and recording numbers— skills lying at the heart of statistics and data analysis. Many kinds of data displays can be used in the primary grades, but they must be used in the service of an investigation, for example, "How much did you grow this year?" "When is your birthday?" "Do you believe in the Easter bunny?" Such questions fascinate first and second graders and can be turned into appropriate exercises in data collection, display, and analysis. As data are collected and displayed, the class can be asked to count along, to make predictions, to compare results: "Which is more, the yes or no column?" "Are there any months with no birthdays?" "Do grownups grow, too?" Provocative questions allow students to begin to talk about what they believe—to argue, to assert, to explain their ideas to each other.

Primary-grade pupils can estimate, count, and represent the number of heads, noses, stomachs, feet, eyes, ears, fingers, and toes in the class. They can collect data to represent their family size, the ages of their siblings, and the ages of their parents. Analysis at this level involves looking at patterns in the data and trying to make sense of the displays.

Young pupils' mathematical work should include much communication. Of course, we have always made birthday charts, but we are just learning that students understand more if such charts become the center of attention for a period of time. Pupils want to count the number of classmates whose birthdays are in each month; they feel bad for the months that are empty; they compare the number of birthdays during the school year with the number of birthdays during the summer. Some students are naturally drawn to looking at the intervals between birthdays in the same month, whereas others prefer to talk about how many candles will be on the birthday cakes they get next time. In all activities, opportunities to

mean. In the seventh and eighth grades, in addition to collecting, exploring, describing, and comparing data, students begin to consider what it means when two different sets of data are related in some way, that is, when one changes the other also exhibits a related change. Throughout, students are involved in summarizing, making conjectures, and building theories to answer the questions that motivated their investigations. Several principles of instruction guide these investigations:

• A spirit of exploration is essential to instruction in statistics and data analysis. Students can be actively engaged in working with real problems in data analysis, but solving real problems with real data is messy. Answers don't come out "even"; data may lend themselves to easy analysis. When dealing with *real* data, students enjoy wrestling with topics and questions for which answers are not obvious.

• Exploring data begins with questions. ("How long can fourth graders typically hold their breath?" "How close can you get to a pigeon?") Questions help students frame active investigations using data either collected or drawn from real-world sources. In the elementary and middle grades, questions that focus on the students themselves or on their immediate surroundings are often of most interest.

• Collecting data needs to be purposeful. ("How much garbage does your family create in a week?" "How does television violence compare with the national crime statistics?") The experience of data collection and analysis is best when it involves questions that *need* answering; this relevance gives purpose to the investigation.

• The use of multiple representations is essential to students' understanding. Students can display data with many different materials, ranging from Unifix cubes and other concrete manipulatives to Post-it notes and to more abstract representations using graphing software. Spreadsheets and databases can be used to organize data, browse through data, and count or calculate summary information for display and analysis.

• Statistical concepts develop from a rich experiential base. Numerous and diverse experiences with collecting, organizing, and analyzing data help students build understandings. For example, students have intuitions

talk and write about the similarities, differences, and patterns are critical to the learning process.

Older primary students need many concrete experiences, also. Second- and third-grade students like to talk about how to define things, and the process of sorting and classifying data intrigues them. They enjoy looking at themselves, collecting data about themselves, and comparing results with others.

Investigations can be incorporated into the more traditional mathematics content taught at this level. For example, students can move beyond a typical, arithmetically oriented measurement curriculum and develop understandings, such as how to use measuring tools, as they become involved in a variety of data-gathering activities.

To appreciate the need for standard units of measure, it is helpful for students to experience the confusion that may result when nonstandard units are used. For instance, what happens when students "pace" their classroom? For this task, they need to practice making paces and deciding where a pace begins and ends. They pace, count, gather, and compare data. Quickly they begin to understand the dilemmas associated with using different-sized paces to measure distances.

At this age, students also seem fascinated with middles: Who is the middle-sized student? Whose foot is middle-sized? Whose pace is middle-sized? Using displays of collected data, they are able to talk about what is middle-sized.

Upper Elementary and Middle School Grades

At the upper elementary and middle school levels, students continue to need a great deal of concrete experience. As in earlier grades, they are interested in questions that focus on themselves. They also are intrigued with what goes on around them and become engaged in both simple and complex issues related to their environment. The use of real data and the

TABLE 1

Brand 1		Brand 2	
Number of raisins	Weight in g	Number of raisins	Weight in g
34	13.5	27	10.1
36	14.5	32	14.2
36	15.1	27	14.0
40	15.8	27	13.5
32	13.9	30	13.9
38	13.8	29	13.8
32	10.5	29	13.5
35	13.7	37	13.4
37	14.2	30	14.5
35	12.0	33	13.5
37	13.7	34	10.8
40	14.9	30	13.5

selection of problems or questions often make it possible to adapt and revisit activities across grade levels. As an example, one problem that appeals to students at this age is exploring the question, How many raisins are in a (half-ounce) box of raisins?

Students guess how many raisins are in a box and then count their data and report results to the class. Students are introduced to a way of sketching their data quickly. A sample graph with a set of raisin data is shown in **figure 2a**. Students spend some time "describing" the data: Where do clusters of data appear? Are any of the data unusual? Do gaps appear in the data? Were students surprised by the results? Why or why not?

Next students use their information to interpret their data and build theories. What if they opened five more boxes—how many raisins do they believe would be in the boxes, given the data they already have? Students can work in small groups to discuss this problem. Several questions arise that they can consider in the course of their discussions. For example, will their predictions be a single number, or can a prediction involve an interval of numbers? Students present their conjectures to the class.

This activity can be extended in a variety of ways. For example, students in the middle school can investigate different brands of raisins. What happens if one brand of raisins pro-

duces a distribution that is quite different from that of another brand of raisins? (See **figs. 2a** and **2b**.) Students may begin to discuss the size of the individual raisins and often extend the activity to include an investigation of weights of raisins. (See **table 1**.) The challenge is to find ways to represent this information visually in some type of display (see **figs. 3a** and **3b**) and then draw conclusions and formulate theories about its behavior.

The Process of Data Analysis

In the last decade, writing teachers have changed their approach to teaching writing. Students' work is treated as communication rather than the creation of objects to be evaluated. If they are to learn to write, students must write often, and, most important, they must write with purpose. Emphasis has shifted away from the creation of a static object (where neatness and spelling count more than the ideas expressed) to focus on the ideas themselves. This new emphasis underlies what is now called the *process approach* to the teaching of writing.

In mathematics, a similar movement has begun. As we begin to see mathematics as a tool for discovering and developing ideas, we can become more flexible about students' invented mathematics, just as writing teachers have become more flexible about students' invented writing. We want to

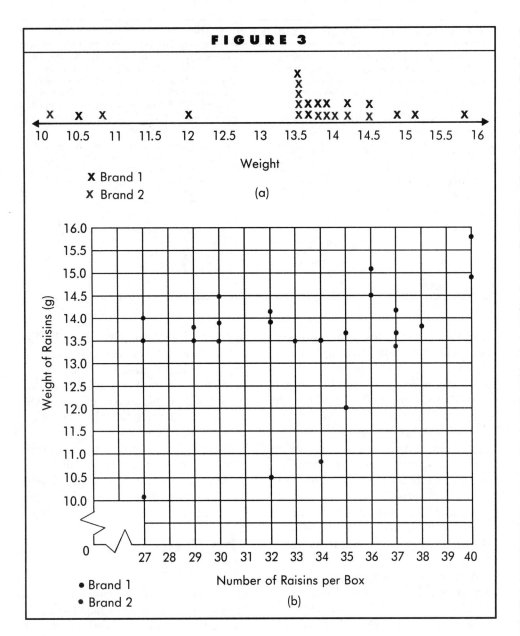

FIGURE 3

Weight

X Brand 1
X Brand 2

(a)

Weight of Raisins (g)

Number of Raisins per Box

• Brand 1
• Brand 2

(b)

through telecommunications or letter writing to pen pals. The provision of an audience makes discovery of patterns and generation of further questions particularly exciting. Other students become interested in nuances of analysis, and theories are discussed and debated. Often, at this time, further research is needed, and the students go back to collect more data.

Finally, *publication* of results may involve making recommendations for action to a responsible person or group. In one class in New York City, the students made a report to the principal after studying the incidence and causes of injuries on their school playground. Their report was accompanied by graphs and charts that the students used to communicate their ideas visually. In another class, students collected data about their class to describe themselves to their pen pals in another location. They used graphs and charts to illustrate the range of various attributes they found in their sample.

Conclusion

Statistics and data analysis are important topics that need to be included throughout the K–8 curriculum. Unlike many topics in mathematics, this area need not be considered as something more to be added to an already full curriculum. Indeed, collecting, displaying, and analyzing data lend themselves to activities that integrate mathematics with other subjects, particularly in the social studies and science curriculum. An excitement ensues in doing real data analysis that can energize the curriculum. We encourage everyone to try it out!

The work of the Used Numbers Project is reflected in this article. Funded by a grant from the National Science Foundation, Technical Education Research Centers, in collaboration with Lesley College, has developed curriculum modules for grades K–6 that focus on data analysis—collecting, organizing, and interpreting quantitative data. Project staff, in addition to authors of this article, are Susan Jo Russell, Janice R. Mokros, Tim Barclay, Toni Stone, and Alana Parkes.

Bibliography

Corwin, Rebecca B., and Susan N. Friel. *Sta-*

encourage our students to view mathematics as something they can use and fiddle with. We want them to work with numbers in a real context, where the questions and the answers make sense to them. Statistics and data analysis help us to furnish the contexts in which students can express themselves and grow mathematically.

Teachers of the process approach to writing talk about phases in the process of writing. Students brainstorm ideas, then write, then revise, and then publish. We can learn much from this approach and can apply it well to the teaching of any problem-solving work in mathematics. Statistics lends itself particularly well to a similar approach.

In the first phase, *brainstorming and planning,* students define their terms and discuss the question to be explored. What question will we explore? How will we get data? How might we record them?

Next comes *data collection and organization.* Students look at compiled data and compose "sketch graphs" to look for patterns and generate hypotheses and questions. They display and redisplay data, trying different methods to give expression to their data and distill information from their displays.

During the *revision* phase, students share their conclusions, theories, and questions with small groups or with the whole class. Some classes have shared their data and their theories

tistics: *Prediction and Sampling (Grades 5–6)*. Palo Alto, Calif.: Dale Seymour Publications, 1990.

Corwin, Rebecca B., and Susan Jo Russell. *Measuring: From Paces to Feet (Grades 3–4)*. Palo Alto, Calif.: Dale Seymour Publications, 1990.

Friel, Susan N., Susan Jo Russell, and Rebecca B. Corwin. *Statistics: Middles, Means, and Inbetweens (Grades 5–6)*. Palo Alto, Calif.: Dale Seymour Publications, 1990.

Graves, Donald. *Writing: Teachers and Children at Work*. Exeter, N.H.: Heinemann, 1983.

National Council of Teachers of Mathematics, Commission on Standards for School Mathematics. *Curriculum and Evaluation Standards for School Mathematics*. Reston, Va.: The Council, 1989.

Russell, Susan Jo, and Rebecca B. Corwin. *Sorting: Groups and Graphs (Grades 2–3)*. Palo Alto, Calif.: Dale Seymour Publications, 1990.

———. *Statistics: The Shape of the Data (Grades 4–6)*. Palo Alto, Calif.: Dale Seymour Publications, 1990.

Russell, Susan Jo, and Susan N. Friel. "Collecting and Analyzing Real Data in the Elementary School Classroom." In *New Directions for Elementary School Mathematics*, 1989 Yearbook of the National Council of Teachers of Mathematics, edited by Paul R. Trafton and Albert P. Shulte. Reston, Va.: The Council, 1989.

Stone, Antoinette, and Susan Jo Russell. *Counting: Ourselves and Our Families (Grades K–1)*. Palo Alto, Calif.: Dale Seymour Publications, 1990. ◆

Probability

Do you think it will rain today?

Do you think we will eat lunch today?

Do you think we will go out for recess today?

What number do you think you will roll?

Is it possible for you to win the game?

These questions are asked by teachers exploring probability with their students. Informal exploration of chance is central to the development of beginning concepts related to probability. Chance is something that most students have experienced in playing games, watching television game shows, and participating in sports. Probability is fun! It should be an important component of any K–8 mathematics program. It should not be one of those "end of year, if I get to it" topics. Probability is of great importance in a number of fields. Although it was founded on principles involving gaming, probability is fundamental to decisions made in business, research, weather forecasting, insurance, sports, and other areas. Theoretically, probability is an application and extension of concepts and skills related to the use of rational numbers (e.g., Stacey has a 1/6 [or

Prepared by **Francis (Skip) Fennell**
Western Maryland College
Westminster, MD 21157

Edited by **Thomas E. Rowan**
Montgomery County Public Schools
Rockville, MD 20850

The Editorial Panel welcomes readers' responses to this article or to any aspect of the Standards *for consideration for publication as an article or as a letter in "Readers' Dialogue."*

about 16.6%] chance of winning the game). Equivalent fractions, ratio, proportion, decimals, and percentage are used in many activities that involve probability. Probability represents real-life mathematics. The study of probability serves as a wonderful opportunity for teachers to ask questions that promote thinking and understanding. Instruction in probability involves experimentation and promotes communication, one of the focal points of the NCTM's *Curriculum and Evaluation Standards for School Mathematics* (*Standards*) (1989). The K–4 and 5–8 Standards involving probability are given here.

K–4 Standard 11: Statistics and Probability

In grades K–4, the mathematics curriculum should include experiments with data analysis and probability so that students can—

- collect, organize, and describe data;
- construct, read, and interpret displays of data;
- formulate and solve problems that involve collecting and analyzing data;
- explore concepts of chance.

5–8 Standard 11: Probability

In grades 5–8, the mathematics curriculum should include explorations of probability in real-world situations so that students can—

- model situations by devising and carrying out experiments or simulations to determine probabilities;
- model situations by constructing a sample space to determine probabilities;
- appreciate the power of using a probability model by comparing experimental results with mathematical expectations;
- make predictions that are based on experimental or theoretical probabilities;
- develop an appreciation for the pervasive use of probability in the real world.

Classroom activities involving probability should be active, involve physical materials, and furnish opportuni-

ties for questioning, problem solution, and discussion. Early on, probability experiments should be relatively easy to complete and verify. For example, given five red and one blue colored-paper circles, a student can intuitively "see" why a red circle is more likely than a blue one to be selected from a paper bag. Probability allows the teacher to develop hypothesis testing in the classroom. Most of the activities that follow compare experimental and theoretical results. Students hypothesize and then test the hypothesis by completing an experiment.

Probability Activities for Grades K–4

It's in the bag

This activity explores chance and examines "fairness." It also introduces certain and impossible events and explores the representation of probability as a fraction.

Show one red, one green, and two blue counters to the class. Ask these questions:

- How many counters do you see?
- How many different colors do you see?

Place the counters in a paper bag. Ask the following questions:

- What color do you think I will probably pull out of the bag? Why?
- Does each color have an equally likely chance of being pulled from the bag? Why or why not?
- How could we make this activity one with equally likely outcomes?
- Can you describe a *certain* event, using these counters? (Pull a counter from the bag.) How about an *impossible* event, using the counters? (Pull a brown counter.)
- What fraction of the balls is green?

- What fraction of the balls is red?
- What fraction of the balls is blue?

Give each small group a paper bag and one red, one green, and two blue counters. Within each group have one student hold the bag, another pull out the counters, and another keep a record of what color was selected. Before each group begins the experiment, ask the students to predict which color will be selected most often in twenty pulls. Record the groups' predictions. Then ask the students to select a counter from their bag, making sure that the recorder tallies the color selected (see **table 1**). The counter is then returned to the bag, which is shaken before another counter is selected. This sequence should be repeated twenty times.

Groups should share their completed tallies with the class. Ask each group the following questions:

- Which color was selected most? Least?
- Did you expect this result? Why or why not?
- Was the number of blue counters selected close to one-half of the total selected?
- Was it possible to pull a red counter from the bag? Why?
- Was it possible to pull a black counter from the bag? Why not?
- (Challenge question) If you pulled a counter from the bag 100 times, how many times would you expect to select a blue counter? A red counter?

Probability and combinations

This activity involves combinations. Students make lists and tree diagrams to determine systematically all possible selections. This activity is intended for use in grades 3–4. It is challenging but can be explored first by representing the cars and interiors with colored markers of two types. Terms such as *random* will need explanation. A popular automobile comes in the following exterior colors: super white, pebble beige, silver, winter blue, red, sand gray, burgundy, charcoal, and super black. The interior colors for these cars are charcoal, blue, burgundy, and beige. Have the students make a list of the car-color options for the interiors and the

---

TABLE 1

Color	Number of draws
Red	
Blue	
Green	

TABLE 2

Exterior colors	Interior colors
Super white (w)	Charcoal (c)
Pebble beige (be)	Blue (b)
Silver (s)	Burgundy (bu)
Winter blue (b)	Beige (be)
Red (r)	
Sand gray (g)	
Burgundy (bu)	
Charcoal (c)	
Super black (bl)	

FIGURE 1

Students can create tree diagrams like the first one shown.

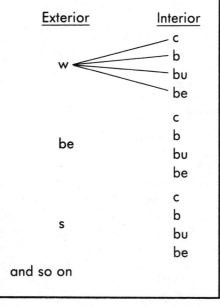

and so on

---

exteriors (see **table 2**).

As the students review their lists, ask the following:

- How many different exterior colors can be selected? Interior colors?
- If someone wanted to buy a red car, what exterior and interior combinations

---

would be possible? (Red and charcoal, red and blue, red and burgundy, and red and beige)

Have the students analyze the exterior and interior color combinations by making a tree diagram to represent the options (see **fig. 1**). Having the students use their tree diagrams, ask these questions:

- How many different exterior and interior color combinations are possible? (36)
- If you want to buy a car with a charcoal interior, from how many different exterior colors can you select? (9)
- If a person selects a car at random, what is the probability that its interior will be blue? (9/36)
- If you want burgundy as a color inside or outside, from how many different combinations can you select? (12)
- Can you find other combinations of colors or other qualities for which using tree diagrams may be helpful in determining the number of options available?
- Can you discover a simple way to determine the number of combinations once you know the number of exterior and interior color options?

What's equally likely?

This activity offers an opportunity to discuss equally likely events. It is intended for use with students in grades K–4. Display a paper cup to the class. Tell them that you are going to drop the cup but that before you do, they should tell how they think the cup might land. Expected responses would be on its side, bottom up, or top up. Drop the cup and discuss the outcome. Give groups of students paper cups. Ask the students to predict the results of dropping their cup ten times. Then have them carry out the experiment and record the results (**table 3**).

After each group has completed a table, ask,

- Did your results match your prediction? Why or why not?
- Why weren't the outcomes in this experiment equally likely?
- Could you make the outcomes equally likely? How?
- What outcome would be certain in this experiment? (That the cup would fall, for example)

TABLE 3

Cup toss

Position	Tally
On side	
Top up	
Bottom up	

TABLE 4

Survey of family size

Family size	Number of families	Fraction	Decimal approximation	Percentage
1	I	1/24	0.042	4
2	IIII	4/24	0.167	17
3	II	2/24	0.083	8
4	IIIIIIIIIII	11/24	0.458	46
5	III	3/24	0.125	13
6	II	2/24	0.083	8
7	I	1/24	0.042	4
8		0/24	0.000	0
Total number of families	24			

TABLE 5

Selection number	Color selected	Probability Fraction	Probability Decimal approximation
1	Red	7/52	0.135
2	Brown	12/51	0.235
3	Brown	11/50	0.22
4	Green	6/49	0.122
5	Orange	8/48	0.167
6	Tan	10/47	0.213
.	.	.	.
.	.	.	.
.	.	.	.
47	Red	1/6	0.167
48	Brown	2/5	0.4
49	Tan	1/4	0.25
50	Green	1/3	0.333
51	Orange	1/2	0.5
52	Brown	1/1	1.0

As the students discuss responses to the questions, take the opportunity to discuss the importance of *equally likely* events. Most paper cups are weighted so that the likely result of a toss is that a cup will land on its side; thus the outcomes of this experiment are theoretically always unequally likely.

Probability Activities for Grades 5–8

Experiments and surveys

A survey often involves a statistical sample. Predictions using probability can be based on sample data. Students in grades 4 and up can use the following activity. Ask students to determine how many people are in each family on their street. An example of such a survey is depicted in **table 4.** Once the survey has been completed and the data organized into a table, questions like the following can be asked:

- How many families were represented in the sample? (24)
- What is the most common family size in the sample? (4)
- On the basis of the sample, what is the probability that a randomly selected family would have four members? (11/24)
- According to the results of this sample, what is the probability that a new family moving into the neighborhood would have more than five members? (3/24)
- What is the likelihood of a family's having less than four members? (7/24)
- If the number of families in the neighborhood tripled, on the basis of the initial sample how many families would have five members? (9)
- Do you think that this information would be true for all neighborhoods? Why or why not?

A next step would be to combine each student's survey data into a class sample and ask similar questions, trying to ascertain if the now-larger sample generates different responses to the questions. Also note that the table has more information than the number of each family's size. Students in grades 4–8 should be encouraged to represent events as fractions and decimals and, when appropriate, as percentages. Such equivalent representation offers real-life rational-number applications. Calculators should be used in creating such equivalents. Some additional topics for a survey are favorite foods, sports, or school subjects; how leisure time is spent; favorite athletic footwear; makes of automobiles on the school parking lot; and others. Use surveys as an opportunity for predicting.

It all depends!

When one event depends on another they are known as *dependent events*. Such events often occur in gaming and real-life settings. Activities with dependent events are appropriate at the middle-grade levels (6–8). This activity also explores certain and impossible events and odds.

Divide the class into groups of three. Pass out bags of counters. Have the students first determine how many counters are in their bag (*note*: Use bags that are not transparent) and how many counters are of each color. Next have the students put the counters back into the bag. Ask each student in the group to take a turn selecting from the bag a counter, which should *not* be returned. As each counter is selected, students should record the color and the probability of its selection and continue selecting counters until the bag is empty. For example, assume the following distribution of counters from a bag: red: 7; tan: 10; brown: 12; green: 6; orange: 8; yellow: 9.

Students should use a calculator to complete a table of the probabilities. They should be encouraged to represent the probability of each selection as a fraction and a decimal. An example of a partial table of the events, using a bag of counters, appears in **table 5.**

Once the selection of counters and the construction of the probability table are completed, ask questions like the following:

- On the basis of our sample bag of counters, which color initially had the highest probability of being selected? The lowest? Would this result be true of all bags? How could we find out?

- What is the probability of selecting a green counter as the fourth selection? Does this result differ from its probability as a first selection?

- How could you determine the probability of selecting a red counter first followed by a brown counter? What is the probability of such a selection? Is this event very likely? Why?

- Which of the events recorded in the table is certain? How do you know? What is meant by a *certain* event? Can you think of an event that would be impossible in this experiment?

- What are the odds against selecting a red counter first? The odds for such a selection?

- After forty-nine selections had been made, what was the probability of selecting a green counter followed by an orange counter as the fiftieth and fifty-first selections, respectively?

- After fifty selections had been completed, what was the probability of selecting an orange counter followed by a brown one as the last two selections? Are these events more likely than selecting a red and brown counter first and second? Why?

TABLE 6

Statistics for the 1990 Baltimore Orioles (through 6/8/90)

Batter	Avg.	G	AB	R	H	2b	3b	HR	RBI	BB
Orsulak	.295	47	166	26	49	7	3	6	31	18
Bradley	.262	49	195	22	51	6	1	1	11	19
Finley	.248	45	153	18	38	7	3	0	10	15
Milligan	.246	53	167	30	41	8	0	6	25	48
B. Ripken	.245	44	139	14	34	6	1	1	11	8
Tettleton	.245	48	163	26	40	9	0	7	30	37
Melvin	.243	35	111	12	27	8	0	2	16	4
Worthington	.243	51	185	22	45	9	0	5	21	22
Gonzales	.218	28	55	7	12	1	0	1	7	7
C. Ripken	.215	55	205	32	44	8	2	7	29	36

Avg.: batting average = hits (H)/at bats (AB); G: number of games; AB: at bats; R: runs; H: hits; 2b: two-base hit, or double; 3b: three-base hit, or triple; HR: home run; RBI: runs batted in; BB: base on balls, or walk

---

The foregoing questions and their responses can serve as a careful development of how dependent events differ from independent events, how to determine such probabilities, how odds are determined and expressed, when events are certain and impossible, and also how the sample size affects probability.

Whereas many, if not most, probability experiences (textbook or supplementary) furnish investigations involving certain and impossible events, many do not deal with the idea of odds. Using our sample bag of counters, we would say that the probability of selecting a red counter first would be 7/52. Seven red counters can be counted in the total of 52. Another way to express this probability is to say that in 45 chances out of 52 the selection of a red counter will not occur. The *odds* against an event's occurring are defined as the ratio of the number of unfavorable events to the number of favorable events. So the odds *against* initially selecting a red counter from our bag are 45 to 7, or 45:7. The odds *for* this event would be 7 to 45, or 7/45, since we are now comparing the number of favorable events to unfavorable events. Students enjoy determining the odds for and against the occurrence of certain events.

An extension activity involving dependent events can use sports to examine one-and-one foul shooting in basketball (see Phillips, Lappan, Win-

ter, and Fitzgerald [1986]). Similarly, board-game applications can include situations like the following:

> You are playing monopoly. Your opponent's marker rests on Marvin Gardens. What is the likelihood of your opponent's rolling a double six, which would allow a second roll of the dice, followed by a two (1 + 1) and landing on Boardwalk, where you have a hotel? (1/36 × 1/36 = 1/1296)

The following real-life scenario involving dependent events may occur on many mornings:

> You have 12 socks in your drawer, 8 of which are blue and 4 are brown. On a rather dark morning you select one sock and then another to make a pair. What is the probability that both socks are brown? (12/132). What are the odds against such a selection? (120 to 12, or 10 to 1)

Sports of all sorts

Sports data can be a rich source of information for predictions of all sorts. Data from prior observations can be analyzed. In the following questions, students have the opportunity to explore probability and odds using the baseball statistics found in **table 6.**

Have the students analyze the batting statistics, then ask questions such as these:

- Given the statistics, what is most likely

for any players listed: getting a hit, making an out, or receiving a base on balls?

- Which player is most likely to get a hit his next time at bat? Least likely?

- Which player is most likely to play the next game? Least likely?

- What is the probability that Tettleton's next hit will be a home run?

- What are the odds against Billy Ripken's getting a hit his next time at bat?

- What is the probability that Bradley will hit a home run his next time at bat?

- What is the probability that Cal Ripken's next hit will be a single?

- If you needed a hit of any type to win a game, who would you like to have bat? Why?

- If you needed an extra-base hit (double, triple, home run) to win a game, who would you like to have bat? Why?

- Suppose that one of the players is having a great game. Do you think the probability of that person's making a hit should be based on the overall statistics or on that game's performance? Explain your response.

Data for individual and group sports can be used for purposes of prediction. The popular rotisserie-league baseball is based on such predictions. Almanacs or newspapers for professional, collegiate, or school-based sports also provide rich probability data.

Real-Life Probability

This manuscript has presented classroom activities that, for the most part, do not involve probabilities associated with flipping coins or rolling dice. Although such activities are valuable, they represent too much of the typical textbook approach to teaching and learning probability. Probability is real-life mathematics. Activities in addition to those presented here that involve world-view applications of probability include experiments involving state lotteries, carnival games, card games, predictions made on the basis of health or accident data (readily available from insurance companies), weather forecasting, and quality control in manufacturing.

In conclusion, NCTM recommends that probability play an active role in the K–8 mathematics curriculum. Probability furnishes an entertaining, exciting backdrop to the learning of key concepts and issues in mathematics, particularly rational-number use. Experiences involving probability should help in the development of rational-number sense. Promote probability in your classroom.

References

Fennell, Francis (Skip). "Ya Gotta Play to Win: A Probability and Statistics Unit for the Middle Grades." *Arithmetic Teacher* 31 (March 1984):26–30.

National Council of Teachers of Mathematics, Commission on Standards for School Mathematics. *Curriculum and Evaluation Standards for School Mathematics*. Reston, Va.: The Council, 1989.

Phillips, Elizabeth, Glenda Lappan, Mary Jean Winter, and William Fitzgerald. *Middle Grade Mathematics Project: Probability*. Menlo Park, Calif.: Addison-Wesley Publishing Co., 1986.

Willerding, Margaret F. *Probability: The Science of Chance*. Chicago: Lyons and Carnahan, 1970. ▼

Patterns, Relations, Functions, and Algebra

5

Patterns, Relationships, and Functions

In the NCTM's *Curriculum and Evaluation Standards for School Mathematics* (1989), function is viewed as both a concept and a process. As a concept, it is the study of regularity and quantification of phenomena, which is the essence of mathematics. As a process, students apply the concept to analyze relationships throughout the curriculum by using tables, graphs, verbal and mathematical rules, and models to represent them.

Despite the fact that "the main body of modern mathematics centers around the concepts of function and limit" (Courant and Robbins 1941, 272), function is a relatively recent idea in the history of mathematics. Descartes introduced the term *function* in 1637, but Galileo (1564–1642) first introduced the idea. Early scientists recognized regularity in nature and concentrated on explaining *why* things happen as they do. Galileo was interested in *how* things happen. By identifying the variables in a situation,

Edited by **Thomas E. Rowan**
Montgomery County Public Schools
Rockville, MD 20850

Prepared by **Hilde Howden**
Mathematics Consultant
Albuquerque, NM 87114

Hilde Howden, now retired, was district mathematics coordinator in the Albuquerque Public Schools, Albuquerque, NM 87125. She is especially interested in the professional development necessary for implementing the NCTM's curricular Standards. *The Editorial Panel welcomes readers' responses to this article or to any aspect of the* Standards.

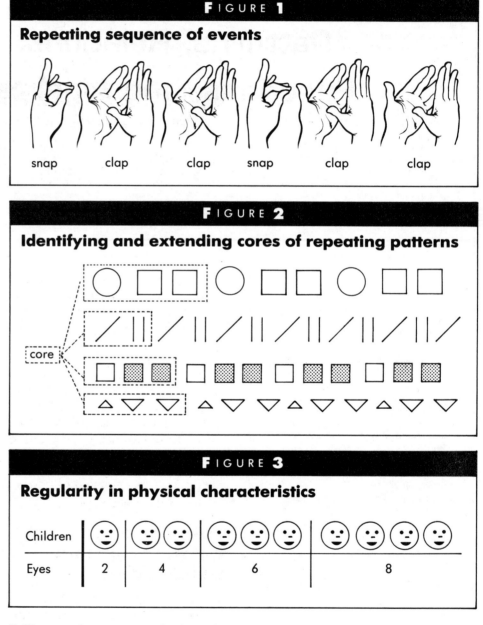

FIGURE 1

Repeating sequence of events

snap   clap   clap   snap   clap   clap

FIGURE 2

Identifying and extending cores of repeating patterns

core

FIGURE 3

Regularity in physical characteristics

Children									
Eyes	2		4			6			8

Galileo sought some quantitative relationship between them (Kline 1953, 185). This exploration of how things happen, or relate, permeates the function standard.

Relationships hold in practically every sphere of life. For example, in science, atmospheric pressure varies with altitude, distance traveled by a falling object varies with time; in business, supply varies with demand, life insurance premiums vary with age of the insured; and in mathematics, linear functions vary with slope, trigono-

TABLE 1

The Function Standard across Levels

TABLE 1

The Function Standard across Levels

Level K–4

STANDARD 13: PATTERN AND RELATIONSHIPS

In grades K–4, the mathematics curriculum should include the study of patterns and relationships so that students can—

♦ recognize, describe, extend, and create a wide variety of patterns;

♦ represent and describe mathematical relationships;

♦ explore the use of variables and open sentences to express relationships.

Level 5–8

STANDARD 8: PATTERNS AND FUNCTIONS

In grades 5–8, the mathematics curriculum should include explorations of patterns and functions so that students can—

♦ describe, extend, analyze, and create a wide variety of patterns;

♦ describe and represent relationships with tables, graphs, and rules;

♦ analyze functional relationships to explain how change in one quantity results in a change in another;

♦ use patterns and functions to represent and solve problems.

Level 9–12

STANDARD 6: FUNCTIONS

In grades 9–12, the mathematics curriculum should include the continued study of functions so that all students can—

♦ model real-world phenomena with a variety of functions;

♦ represent and analyze relationships using tables, verbal rules, equations, and graphs;

♦ translate among tabular, symbolic, and graphical representations of functions;

♦ recognize that a variety of problem situations can be modeled by the same type of function;

♦ analyze the effects of parameter changes on the graphs of functions;

and so that, in addition, college-intending students can—

♦ understand operations on, and the general properties and behavior of, classes of functions.

FIGURE 4

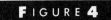

Recreating regularity with concrete objects

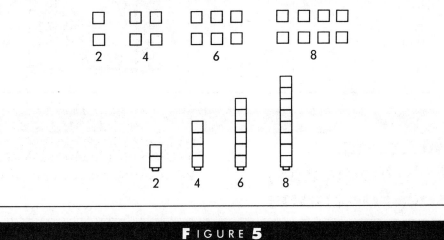

FIGURE 5

Pattern of growing rectangles

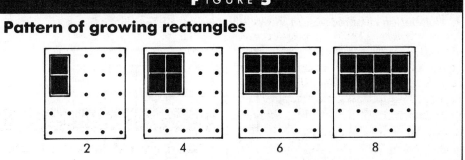

metric functions vary with angle measure. Such applications of function enable students to see mathematics as an integrated whole, to link conceptual and procedural knowledge, to recognize relationships among different topics in mathematics, and to re-late mathematics to other disciplines.

Both aspects, concept and process, are essential to understanding function, and both aspects are identified in specific standards at each of levels K–4, 5–8, and 9–12 (see **table 1**).

At each level the standard builds on the preceding levels. The central theme is how things are related at each of the levels. The *Standards* document furnishes many examples of this building process; the examples in this article synthesize the discussions and illustrate the difference in emphasis within the building process.

Patterns and Relationships in Grades K–4

In the early grades, the focus is on regularity in events, shapes, designs, and sets of numbers. Recognition of regularity can be as simple as telling what comes next in a repeating sequence of events (**fig. 1**) or identifying and extending cores of repeating patterns (see **fig. 2**).

Patterns involve many attributes, such as color, shape, direction, orientation, and number. Seeing multiple representations of the same pattern helps students to focus on its structure. For example, the five patterns in **figures 1** and **2** have the same structure, which can be represented verbally as one / one, two / one / one, two / . . . or symbolically as 1, 1–2, 1, 1–2, ...

Children can be encouraged to look for generalizable patterns: one child has two eyes, two children have four eyes, three children have six eyes, and four children have eight eyes, as tabulated in **figure 3**. Recreating this pattern with concrete objects, such as tiles and Unifix cubes, offers students opportunities to generalize (see **fig. 4**). Questions like "How many cubes are in the next tower?" and "How many cubes are in the next tower after that?" help children to verbalize a rule, such as "Add two each time," for obtaining succeeding elements of the pattern. They recognize that the same rule applies when they "cover" growing rectangles on a geoboard, as illustrated in **figure 5**.

TABLE 2

Recording Calculator Input and Output

Number of times $=$ is entered	1	2	3	4	5	6	7	8	9	10	11	12	50	80	100
Display	2	4	6	8	10	12	14	16	18	20	22	24			

FIGURE 6

Rule: □ + □ or 2 × □

Number of Wheels Varies with Number of Bicycles

Number of bicycles	1	2	3	4	5	6	7	8	...	23
Number of wheels	2	4	6	8	10	12	14	16	...	46

Number on Hundreds Chart Varies with Number of Two-Place Skips

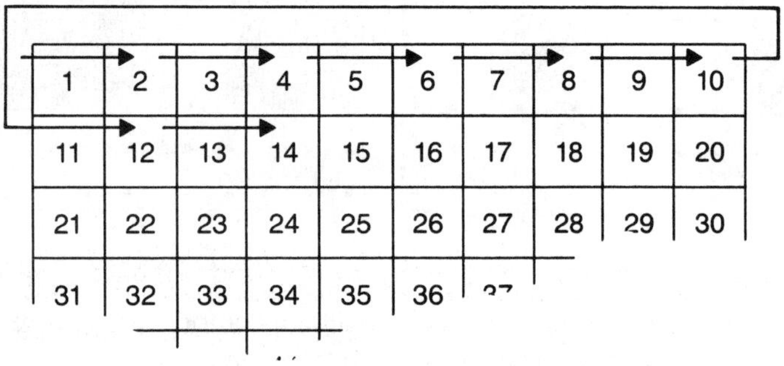

FIGURE 7

Rule: □ + □ + □ or 3 × □

Number of Wheels Varies with Number of Tricycles

Number of tricycles	1	2	3	4	5	6	7	8	...	23
Number of wheels	3	6	9	12	15	18	21	24	...	69

Number on Hundreds Chart Varies with Number of Three-Place Skips

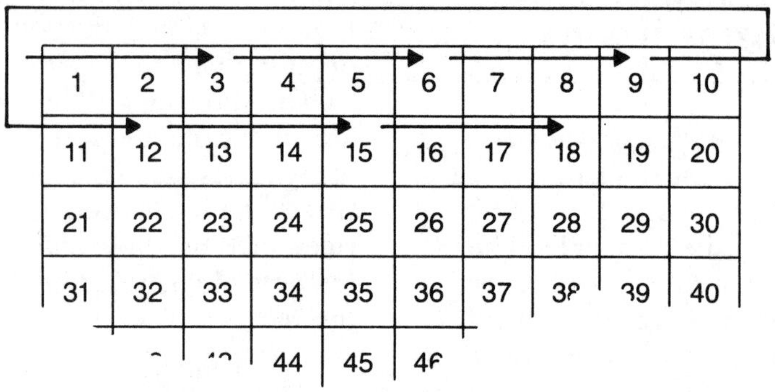

TABLE 3

Rule: 2 × □ (Even Numbers)

Number of element	Value of element
1	2
2	4
3	6
4	8
5	10

Using the addition function on a calculator allows students to apply this rule many times.

Example

Two students work together. On a calculator on which $\boxed{+}$ $\boxed{2}$ has been previously entered, one student repeatedly enters $\boxed{=}$. The second student records the resulting displays in a prepared table (see **table 2**).

Faced with the problem of extending the table without using a calculator, students intuitively develop the idea of a functional relationship. Some students will recognize that each display entry is equal to its corresponding entry added to itself; others will recognize each display entry as the double of its corresponding entry; and still others will say, "Multiply by two." On the basis of these observations, the pattern rule can be revised as □ + □ or as 2 × □. Whether "□" is interpreted as "any number," "place holder," or "box to be filled," the groundwork is established for future understanding of the concept of variable.

Searching their environment for relationships that obey a given rule, such as □ + □ or 2 × □ (see **fig. 6**), reinforces both the understanding of the relationship and the concept of variable. Such a search also leads to extensions of relationships and their rules, as illustrated in **figure 7.**

By comparing the pattern of even-numbered tiles with a pattern whose elements are odd numbers of tiles, as in **figure 8,** students recognize that in both patterns succeeding elements are generated by adding two tiles, but the values of the elements are different. Tabulating the number of each element and its value, as in **tables 3** and

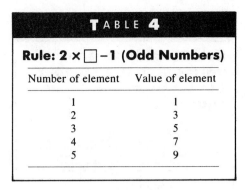

TABLE 4

Rule: 2 × □ − 1 (Odd Numbers)

Number of element	Value of element
1	1
2	3
3	5
4	7
5	9

4, helps students to express their rules mathematically.

Using their rules to predict the value of an element when given its number introduces students to the power of mathematics, and verifying their predictions by building tile models or by successive additions of two on a calculator convinces students that mathematics makes sense.

Patterns and Functions in Grades 5–8

In grades 5–8, the study of patterns builds on these experiences. Here the emphasis centers on informal analysis that employs multiple representations, such as concrete models, data tables, graphs, expressions, equations, and verbal descriptions. From such representations, students identify variables, recognize that changes in one variable affect changes in another, and begin to develop proportional thinking. The following example illustrates such an informal analysis.

Students look for relationships as they identify and extend a tile model of the growing pattern of squares (see **fig. 9**). Three relationships are immediately apparent:

1. The number of tiles that must be added to a given square to construct the next square varies with the number of tiles on a side of the given square.

2. The number of tiles in the area of a square varies with the number of tiles on a side of the square.

3. The perimeter of a square varies with the number of tiles on a side of the square.

The variables in the first relationship

FIGURE 8

Comparing patterns with a similar structure

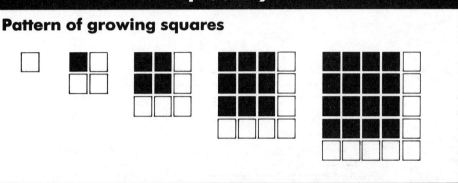

FIGURE 9

Pattern of growing squares

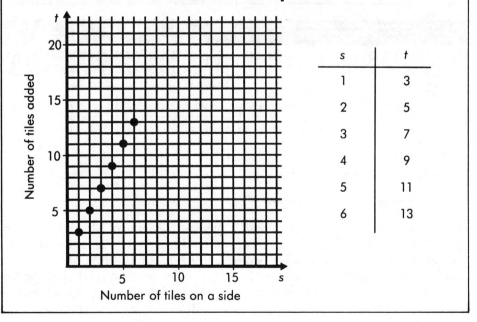

FIGURE 10

Relationship 1: Number of tiles added varies with the number of tiles on a side of the square.

s	t
1	3
2	5
3	7
4	9
5	11
6	13

can be identified as s, the number of tiles along each side of a square, and t, the number of tiles that need to be added to make the next square. As s increases, so does t, but t increases more rapidly than s does. For every change of one unit in s the change in t is two, giving the proportional relationship

$$\frac{\text{change in } s}{\text{change in } t} = \frac{1}{2}.$$

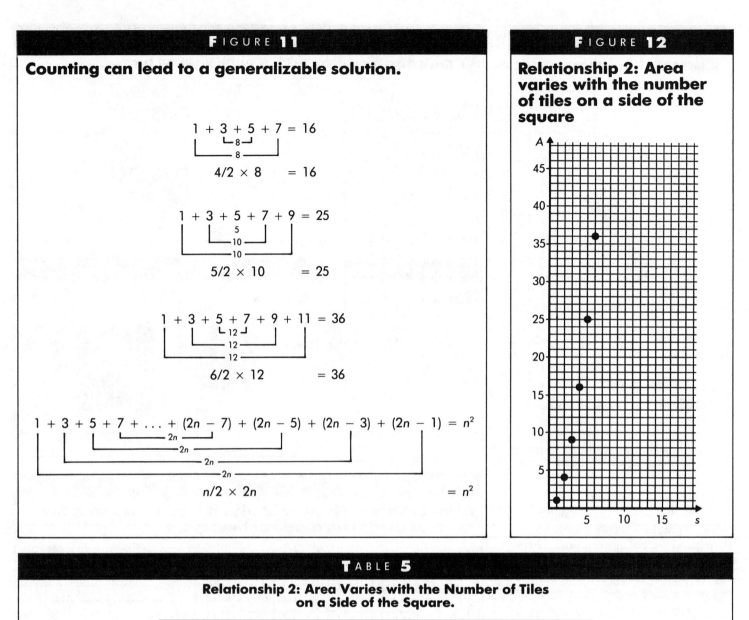

FIGURE 11

Counting can lead to a generalizable solution.

$$1 + 3 + 5 + 7 = 16$$

$$4/2 \times 8 = 16$$

$$1 + 3 + 5 + 7 + 9 = 25$$

$$5/2 \times 10 = 25$$

$$1 + 3 + 5 + 7 + 9 + 11 = 36$$

$$6/2 \times 12 = 36$$

$$1 + 3 + 5 + 7 + \ldots + (2n - 7) + (2n - 5) + (2n - 3) + (2n - 1) = n^2$$

$$n/2 \times 2n = n^2$$

FIGURE 12

Relationship 2: Area varies with the number of tiles on a side of the square

TABLE 5

Relationship 2: Area Varies with the Number of Tiles on a Side of the Square.

s (Number of tiles on a side)	1	2	3	4	5	6
A (Number of tiles in square)	1	4	9	16	25	36

$$1 + 3 \qquad 1 + 3 + 5 \qquad 1 + 3 + 5 + 7 + 9$$
$$1 + 3 + 5 + 7 \qquad 1 + 3 + 5 + 7 + 9 + 11$$

Recording the data in tabular and graphic format (see **fig. 10**) reveals the entries for *t* to be successive odd numbers and suggests the mathematical relationship $t = 2s + 1$, which can be checked by building more elements in the tile model.

In the second relationship, the variables are *s*, the number of tiles on a side, and *A*, the area. Students can approach the problem of finding the area of each square in two ways: by counting tiles in the tile model or by finding the sum of all tiles added to preceding squares from the table of *s* and *t* values (see **table 5**).

The first method reinforces the formula for the area of a square as $A = s^2$. However, the second method suggests an unexpected relationship, that is, the sum of consecutive odd numbers is equal to the square of the number of addends in the sum. Although the study of arithmetic series is a traditional component of a formal algebra course, an informal introduction here illustrates how counting can lead to a generalizable solution as developed in **figure 11**. Such developments take the mystery out of mathematics and help students to see that mathematics makes sense. Thus, by either method, the relationship can be expressed mathematically as $A = s^2$. In this relationship, *A* increases as *s* increases, but the increase is not constant, as it was in the first relationship. This fact is evident from its graph in **figure 12**.

Relationship 3: Perimeter varies with the number of tiles on a side of the square.

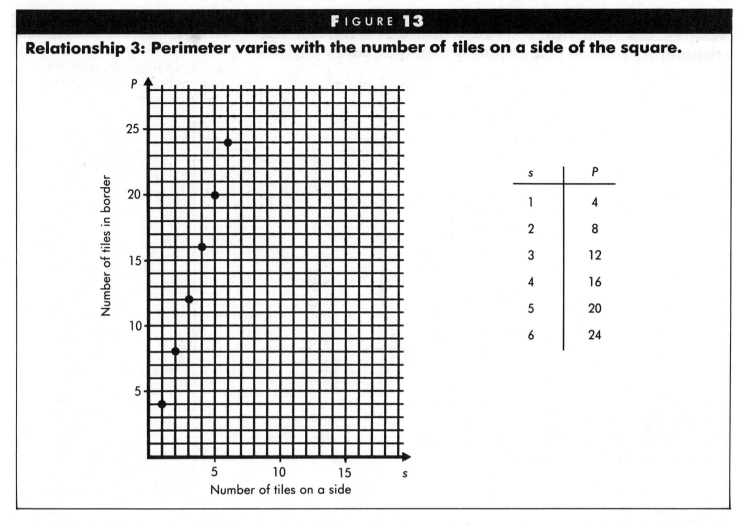

s	P
1	4
2	8
3	12
4	16
5	20
6	24

The third relationship is similar to the first; each successive increase of one unit in s results in an increase of a constant number of units, four, in the perimeter P, as shown in **figure 13,** so that $s/P = \frac{1}{4}$, or $P = 4s$.

An analysis of the combined graph of the three relationships reinforces their likenesses and differences. It also presents a natural opportunity for an intuitive introduction to continuity and limits. With squares of paper that are one-half, one-fourth, one-eighth, and one-tenth of the length s on a side, students can model the pattern of shrinking, rather than growing, squares. The added benefit of such an extension is the realization that computational skills with fractions and decimals have practical applications in mathematics, as illustrated in **figure 14.**

In a similar analysis of the pattern of growing triangles (see **fig. 15**), students make some unexpected discoveries. After their experience with the growing-squares pattern, students generally predict that P, the perimeter of each triangle, is three units more than the perimeter of the triangle it follows in the pattern. That is, $P = 3s$. However, they are surprised to see that the number of tiles added to each element of the pattern and the area relationship are exactly the same as for the growing-squares pattern.

Experiences with concrete materials, graphs, and pictorial representations help students to visualize characteristics of all sorts of relationships from their everyday experiences and help them to recognize that in generating, organizing, and analyzing data to identify and generalize patterns, mathematics applies to any situation that can be quantified.

Summary

The exploration of patterns, relationships, and functions is a thread that runs through the entire *Standards* document as students encounter regularities in all of mathematics, from counting and computation to underpinnings of calculus. In addition, each level includes a specific functions standard that builds on preceding experiences.

At level K–4, the focus is on regularity in events, shapes, designs, and sets of numbers. Students recognize, extend, describe, and create a wide variety of patterns; identify and describe how they are related; and use open sentences to express the relationships. These experiences are extended at the 5–8 level as students represent relationships in various formats to identify variables and recognize how change in one variable affects change in another. At this level, students begin to use patterns and functions to represent and solve problems. The focus at the 9–12 level becomes more abstract as students use functions to model real-world phenomena and analyze the effects of

FIGURE 14

Comparing relationships in the growing-squares pattern

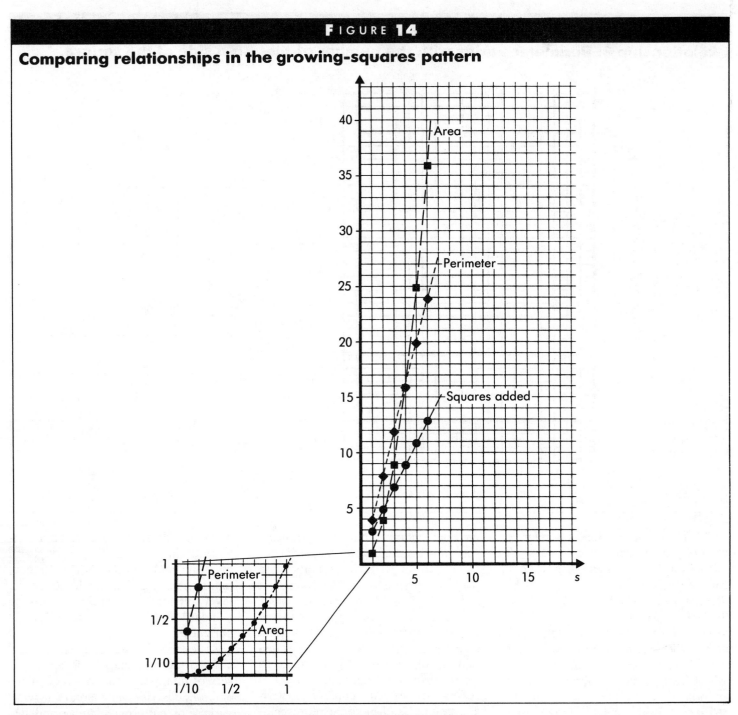

FIGURE 15

Pattern of growing triangles

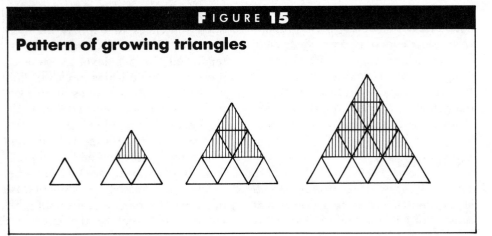

parametric changes on the graphs of functions and recognize general properties and behavior of classes of functions.

References

Courant, Richard, and Herbert Robbins. *What Is Mathematics?* New York: Oxford University Press, 1941.

Kline, Morris. *Mathematics in Western Culture.* New York: Oxford University Press, 1953.

National Council of Teachers of Mathematics, Committee on Standards for School Mathematics. *Curriculum and Evaluation Standards for School Mathematics.* Reston, Va.: The Council, 1989. ❦

Teaching Informal Algebra

Algebra is described in the NCTM's *Curriculum and Evaluation Standards for School Mathematics* (1989, 150) as "the language through which most of mathematics is communicated." For many years *algebra* has often referred to a single course or two featuring manipulative skills and punctuated by other courses called *prealgebra or geometry.* In the spirit of the *Curriculum and Evaluation Standards*, it is more appropriate to think of algebra as a cohesive body of concepts, closely connected to other branches of mathematics, in which manipulative skills play a supporting rather than star role. In this context, the distinction between prealgebra and algebra is less apparent. Rather, a gradual building from informal to formal concepts takes place over most of the K–12 curriculum. In the continuing series on implementing the *Standards*, this article presents suggestions for developing algebraic concepts beginning in the early grades.

Representing Relationships

The beginnings of algebra may not look much like what we now call algebra. For

Prepared by **James E. Schultz**
Ohio State University
Columbus, OH 43210

Edited by **Thomas E. Rowan**
Montgomery County Public Schools
Rockville, MD 20850

The Editorial Panel welcomes readers' responses to this article or to any aspect of the Curriculum and Evaluation Standards for consideration for publication as an article or as a letter in "Readers' Dialogue."

FIGURE 1

Pupils complete the pattern by finishing the drawing of the next house.

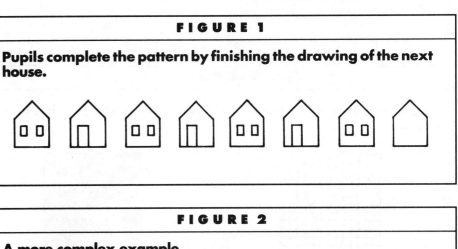

FIGURE 2

A more complex example

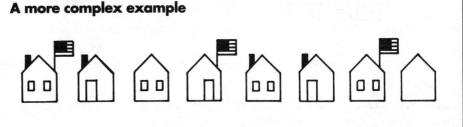

FIGURE 3

Students make the next three shapes.

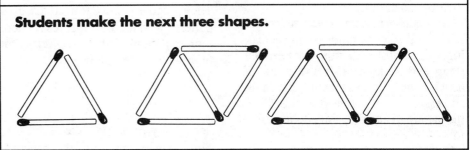

example, have very young pupils complete patterns like the one in **figure 1,** giving the instruction that they should "finish drawing the next house." As pupils communicate their reasoning with statements like "every other house has a door," they are beginning to develop "the language through which most of mathematics is communicated," namely, the language of algebra. It is worth noting that at

this level ordinary language rather than abstract symbols is used to describe patterns. (Teachers should certainly allow for the possibility in the example that some pupils may want to break the pattern, so that every other house does not have a door!)

Patterns can increase in complexity, as in **figure 2,** leading to a discussion of questions like "Does the next house have

FIGURE 4

Numerical representation of
7 × 13 = 7 × 10 + 7 × 3

Algebraic representation of
a (b + c) = ab + ac

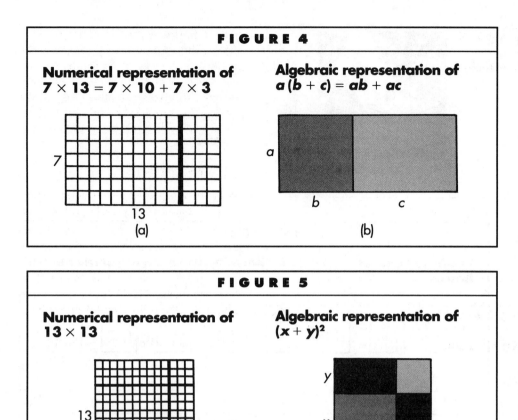

(a)

(b)

FIGURE 5

Numerical representation of
13 × 13

Algebraic representation of
(x + y)²

(a)

(b)

FIGURE 6

An extension to volume for
(x + y)³

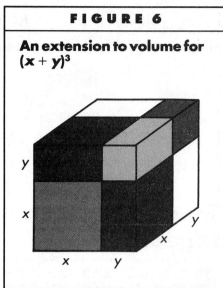

a flag? Why? Does it have a door? On which side of the house is it? Why do you think so? Does anyone disagree? How else could we make the houses different?" Finally pupils could be asked to make up their own patterns.

As students mature, other patterns can lead them to communicate in increasingly more abstract terms. For example, Pegg and Redden (1990) describe an activity with matches that they have used successfully with twelve-year-olds. Given the pattern in **figure 3,** students are asked to—

1. make the next three shapes;
2. find how many matches are needed for the fifth and sixth shapes;
3. find out how many matches are needed for the eleventh shape; and
4. state how the pattern grows.

Pegg and Redden reported that even with no prior instruction with patterns, all pupils achieved success with little or no assistance from the teacher.

Students later summarize results in charts like this:

Number of triangles 1 2 3 . . .
Number of matches 3 5 7 . . .

They gradually move toward discussing patterns with increasingly less concrete representations. Subsequent representations include ideagrams like

and finally equations like $m = 2t + 1$. Such a development of the concept of equation is consistent with the *Curriculum and Evaluation Standards*.

The gradual building of the concept of variable is also supported by Demana and Leitzel (1988) in an outgrowth of the Approaching Algebra Numerically Project. In this project seventh- and eighth-grade students build the concept of variable through making tables and graphs, with calculators playing a major role. For example, compound-interest problems are

explored in depth in tables and graphs before students ever see equations or formulas, with the computations being performed on calculators. Only after considerable experience with tables and graphs do students work with abstract representations for equations, as illustrated later in "Solving Equations."

Area models are another tool for visualization of algebraic concepts. For example, students can move from numerical representations like $7 \times 13 = 7 \times 10 + 7 \times 3$ to algebraic representations like $a(b + c) = ab + ac$, as shown in **figure 4.** In **figure 4b** note that the area is $a(b + c)$ if viewed as one rectangle, whereas it is $ab + ac$ if viewed as the sum of two rectangles.

Later students can move from numerical representations like 13×13 to algebraic representations like

$$(x + y)^2 = x^2 + 2xy + y^2,$$

as shown in **figure 5.** In **figure 5b** note that the area is $(x + y)^2$ if viewed as one square, whereas it is $x^2 + 2xy + y^2$ if viewed as the sum of one square, two rectangles, and another square. See Schultz (forthcoming) for ideas about using area models in teaching operations.

This approach can later be extended to volume models for expressions like $(x + y)^3$, as suggested by **figure 6,** where the volume can be viewed as one cube with dimensions $(x + y)^3$ or as the sum of a cube with dimensions x^3, three rectangular prisms of dimensions x^2y, three rectangular prisms of dimensions xy^2, and a cube with dimensions y^3.

FIGURE 7

A one-step solution using cups and chips

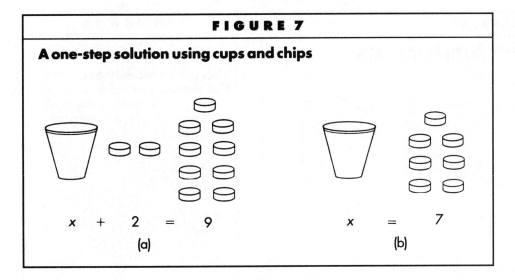

$x + 2 = 9$

(a)

$x = 7$

(b)

FIGURE 8

A two-step solution using cups and chips

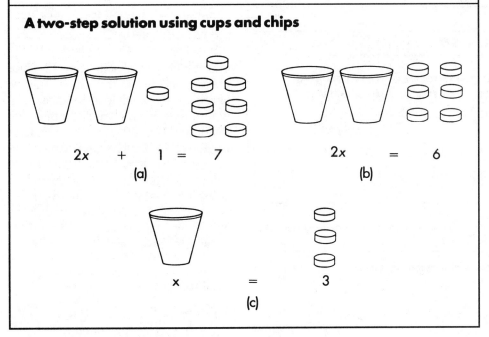

$2x + 1 = 7$

(a)

$2x = 6$

(b)

$x = 3$

(c)

Solving Equations

The foregoing examples show how algebraic relationships can be expressed using a variety of representations, including concrete objects, pictures, ideagrams, tables, graphs, and finally equations. The perils of rushing too quickly to abstract representations are illustrated in a classroom anecdote reported by Mahaffey (conversation with author). A student asked to "find x in each equation," such as "$x + 2 = 9$," simply circled all the x's. He had found them indeed! Although this anecdote may generate a chuckle, it reveals the level of understanding of the concept of variable that many students have when they are rushed into solving equations symbolically.

Students can also learn the concepts behind solving equations in more concrete ways. For example, the equation $x + 2 = 9$ can be represented concretely using cups and chips as shown in **figure 7a.** Some teachers place chips in a cup and seal them from view by placing a second cup inside the first. To "find x" (i.e., solve the equation), students can remove two chips from each side of the equation to achieve the result shown in **figure 7b.**

The solution of a two-step equation is shown in **figure 8.** Beginning with the equation $2x + 1 = 7$ in **figure 8a,** students subtract 1 from each side to obtain $2x =$ 6, as in **figure 8b,** and then divide each side of this equation by 2 to obtain the solution $x = 3$, as in **figure 8c.** Earlier experiences with these concrete representations can give students a referent for solving equations as the representations become more abstract and more complex.

Applications

Applications can be used to make algebraic concepts more meaningful, as well as more interesting. For example, information regarding direct flights can be gleaned from an airlines timetable, especially one that gives distances as well as time. For example, a Delta Airlines timetable gives the following information:

Nonstop Flights from Atlanta

City	Miles	Minutes
Birmingham, Ala.	134	41
Boston	946	140
Chicago	596	102
Columbus, Ohio	446	83
Dallas	731	119
Denver	1208	175
Los Angeles	1946	250
Minneapolis	906	150
Washington	543	92
Philadelphia	665	112

If these data are graphed in a scattergram, they are fit quite well by a straight line, as shown in **figure 9.** The graph of this line could be sketched by students or drawn by a statistical software package. In this application, the notion of a linear relationship becomes meaningful, since the slope of the line (about 8.6 miles per minute) is the speed of the airplane and the x- intercept (about 32 minutes) is the time spent for taxiing. Students can benefit from relating to these notions before moving to more abstract representations for slope and intercept. Besides making the algebra more meaningful, such examples also build connections to statistics.

Use of Technology

Calculators, graphing utilities on graphing calculators or computers, and spreadsheets, in addition to such statistical packages as mentioned in the preceding example, can be used to enhance instruction in algebra. For example, to determine

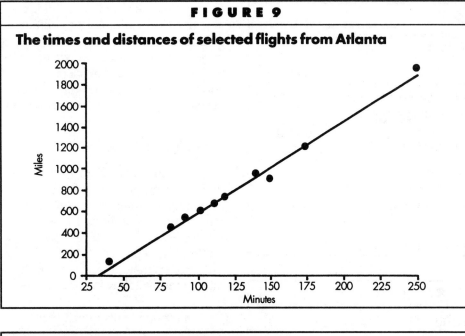

FIGURE 9

The times and distances of selected flights from Atlanta

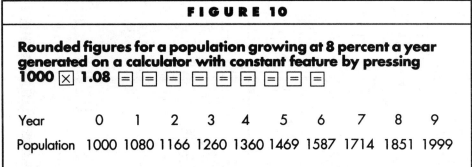

FIGURE 10

Rounded figures for a population growing at 8 percent a year generated on a calculator with constant feature by pressing 1000 ☒ 1.08 ⊟ ⊟ ⊟ ⊟ ⊟ ⊟ ⊟ ⊟ ⊟

Year	0	1	2	3	4	5	6	7	8	9
Population	1000	1080	1166	1260	1360	1469	1587	1714	1851	1999

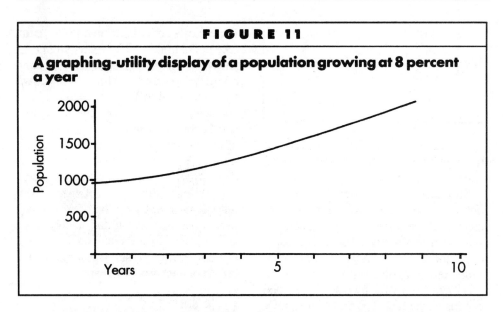

FIGURE 11

A graphing-utility display of a population growing at 8 percent a year

FIGURE 12

Using a spreadsheet to find the dimensions of a rectangular pen of perimeter 100 meters that yield the maximum area

	A	B	C
1	Length	Width	Area
2	5	45	225
3	10	40	400
4	15	35	525
5	20	30	600
6	25	25	625
7	30	20	600
8	35	15	525
9	40	10	400
10	45	5	225

a spreadsheet like that in **figure 12.** Since the perimeter is 100, they can see that the length and the width total 50, so they can write a spreadsheet formula for the width in column B as 50 minus the length in column A, and for the area in column C as the length in column A times the width in column B. The natural and highly useful skills involved in writing these spreadsheet formulas lead quite naturally to writing algebraic expressions like $50 - l$ for width and lw for area.

Conclusion

This brief article suggests a few of the ways in which concrete materials, pictures, graphs, calculators, and computers can be used to support concept building in algebra so that "the language through which most of mathematics is communicated" need not be a foreign language to students.

References

Demana, Franklin D., and Joan R. Leitzel. *Getting Ready for Algebra, Levels 1 and 2.* Lexington, Mass.: D. C. Heath & Co., 1988.

National Council of Teachers of Mathematics, Commission on Standards for School Mathematics. *Curriculum and Evaluation Standards for School Mathematics.* Reston, Va.: The Council, 1989.

Pegg, John, and Edward Redden. "Procedures for, and Experiences in, Introducing Algebra in New South Wales." *Mathematics Teacher* 83 (May 1990):386–91.

Schultz, James E. "Area Models Spanning the Mathematics of Grades 3–9." Forthcoming. ▰

how many years it takes for the population of a city to double if it is growing at a rate of 8 percent a year from an original population of 1000, a calculator with a constant feature (**fig. 10**) or a graphing utility (**fig. 11**) can be used to display the growth. In this setting the technology helps to visualize the mathematical relationship between time and population.

Spreadsheets too can help build concepts in algebra. For example, in trying to find the dimensions of a rectangular pen using 100 meters of fencing to achieve the maximum area, students might construct

AN ANNOTATED BIBLIOGRAPHY OF ARITHMETIC TEACHER ARTICLES RELATED TO THE STANDARDS

Themes That Cut across Mathematics (problem solving, communication, reasoning, connections, assessment)

Arithmetic Teacher 39 (February 1992). Focus issue on assessment.

Articles on linking assessment with instruction, alternative forms of assessment, self-evaluation, using manipulatives on tests, and suggestions for assessing cooperative problem solving.

Barnett, Carne S. "Ideas." *Arithmetic Teacher* 38 (January 1991): 26–33.

Sneakers are investigated, graphed, and measured. Presents opportunities for conjectures and verification.

Bitner, Joe, and M. Elizabeth Partridge. "'Stocking Up' on Mathematics Skills." *Arithmetic Teacher* 38 (March 1991): 4–7.

Using stock-market statistics, students examine real-life applications of fractions and percents.

Bohan, Harry. "Mathematical Connections: Free Rides for Kids." *Arithmetic Teacher* 38 (November 1990): 10–14.

Explains a strategy for connecting bits of mathematical knowledge and building a hierarchy of related skills.

Brown, Sue. "Integrating Manipulatives and Computers in Problem-solving Experiences." *Arithmetic Teacher* 38 (October 1990): 8–10.

Shows how manipulatives can enhance understanding when used with technology; offers a variety of activities.

Burns, Marilyn. "Introducing Division through Problem-solving Experiences." *Arithmetic Teacher* 38 (April 1991): 14–18.

Cooperative groups in third grade solve several division problems, justify their answers, and describe their solutions verbally or in writing.

Cangelosi, James S. "Language Activities That Promote Awareness of Mathematics." *Arithmetic Teacher* 36 (December 1988): 6–9.

Gives examples of first-, fourth-, and sixth-grade classes that use writing and speaking about mathematics to heighten students' awareness of mathematics applications in the real world.

Cemen, Pamala Byrd. "Developing a Problem-solving Lesson." *Arithmetic Teacher* 37 (October 1989): 14–19.

Offers suggestions to help prepare fourth- and fifth-grade lessons on problem solving that include several problems, as well as questions that can be asked to help students solve the problems.

Clark, H. Clifford, and Marvin N. Nelson. "Evaluation: Be More Than a Scorekeeper." *Arithmetic Teacher* 38 (May 1991): 15–17.

Describes classroom techniques for informal assessment as a part of instruction. Discusses immediate feedback, students' analyses of their errors, and cooperative-group work as components of such assessment.

Cobb, Paul, Erna Yackel, Terry Wood, Grayson Wheatley, and Graceann Merkel. "Research into Practice: Creating a Problem-solving Atmosphere." *Arithmetic Teacher* 36 (September 1988): 46–47.

Relates research on attempts to create a problem-solving atmosphere in which children can explain and justify solutions to problems.

Davis, Robert B. "Research into Practice: Giving Pupils Tools for Thinking." *Arithmetic Teacher* 38 (January 1991): 23–25.

Discusses the concept of negative numbers as a tool for children in invented arithmetic; suggests a technique to make negative numbers meaningful to young children.

Burns, 1991

Maria has 5 cars. Bill has 8 cars. How many more cars does Bill have?

NCTM *Standards*, p. 41

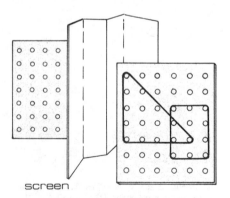

What Am I?

I have 3 or 4 sides.
All my angles are equal.
My sides are not all equal.

Who Am I?

I am an even number.
I am more than 20 and less than 30.
I am not 25.
The sum of my digits is 8.

NCTM *Standards,* p. 30

Here are some examples of calculator-active problems based on problems and suggestions found in the NCTM's curriculum standards.

Example 1. I have four coins; each coin is either a penny, a nickel, a dime, or a quarter.

a) If altogether the coins are worth a total of forty-one cents, how many pennies, nickels, dimes, and quarters might I have? Is more than one answer possible?

b) What could be the maximum value of the four coins? The minimum value?

c) If I have exactly one penny and one dime, what could be the maximum value of the four coins? The minimum value?

d) What are all the possible total values of the four coins?

Harvey, 1991

screen

Arrangement of geoboards for assessing speaking and listening skills

NCTM *Standards,* p. 215

Davison, David M., and Daniel L. Pearce. "Using Writing Activities to Reinforce Mathematics Instruction." *Arithmetic Teacher* 35 (April 1988): 42–45.

Explores ways in which teachers can use writing during mathematics instruction.

Ford, Margaret I. "The Writing Process: A Strategy for Problem Solvers." *Arithmetic Teacher* 38 (November 1990): 35–38.

Recommends strategies for helping students learn to write problems; includes stages of generating ideas, writing drafts, and editing.

Fortunato, Irene, Deborah Hecht, Carol Kehr Tittle, and Laura Alvarez. "Metacognition and Problem Solving." *Arithmetic Teacher* 39 (December 1991): 38–40.

Describes results of a survey of seventh graders' awareness of the cognitive processes they use in problem solving. The questionnaire could give teachers insight into strengths and weaknesses of students and suggest future directions in problem-solving activities.

Frank, Martha L. "Problem Solving and Mathematical Beliefs." *Arithmetic Teacher* 35 (January 1988): 32–34.

Discusses beliefs middle school students hold about problem solving and the implications these beliefs have for teaching.

Goldman, Phyllis H. (March 1990). See entry under ***"Number."***

Harvey, John G. "Teaching Mathematics with Technology: Using Calculators in Mathematics Changes Testing." *Arithmetic Teacher* 38 (March 1991): 52–54.

Suggests ways in which test items should be altered for use with calculators to lead to greater emphasis on applications and pattern and less emphasis on rote computation.

Hoeffner, Karl, Monica Kendall, Cheryl Stellenwerf, Pixie Thames, and Patricia Williams. "Teaching Mathematics with Technology: Problem Solving with a Spreadsheet." *Arithmetic Teacher* 38 (November 1990): 52–56.

Lists activities for middle school students that use real-life data to explore costs of a party or patterns in interest rates and payments.

Kamii, Constance, and Barbara Ann Lewis. "Achievement Tests in Primary Mathematics: Perpetuating Lower-Order Thinking." *Arithmetic Teacher* 38 (May 1991): 4–9.

Argues that since achievement tests tap mainly the knowledge of symbols, they do not test children's understanding, logical reasoning ability, or knowledge of relationships.

Knecht, Paul S. "Making Mathematics Meaningful with M&Ms." *Arithmetic Teacher* 38 (May 1991): 50–51.

Presents preschoolers and kindergartners with problems relating to the sorting, counting, and sharing of candy bits. Discusses possible extensions.

Labinowicz, Ed. "Assessing for Learning: The Interview Method." *Arithmetic Teacher* 35 (November 1987): 22–23.

Outlines different aspects of interviewing to help teachers use this method to learn about students' strengths and weaknesses.

Liedtke, Werner. "One Point of View: Let's Talk about Talking Mathematics." *Arithmetic Teacher* 35 (April 1988): 2.

Contends that letting children talk and listening to them can lead to valuable insights into their thinking.

Long, Madeleine J., and Meir Ben-Hur. "Informing Learning through the Clinical Interview." *Arithmetic Teacher* 38 (February 1991): 44–46.

Suggests "flexible" interviews to encourage verbalization and provide diagnostic data.

McClintic, Susan V. "Conservation—a Meaningful Gauge for Assessment." *Arithmetic Teacher* 35 (February 1988): 12–14.

Discusses ways in which nonconserving children can benefit from counting, one-to-one matching, and seriation tasks.

Moniuszko, Linda K. "'Reality Math'." *Arithmetic Teacher* 39 (September 1991): 10–16.

Details projects that actively involve middle school students, including choosing and "paying for" a new car and planning a Thanksgiving dinner. Sample worksheets are included.

Newman, Claire M., and Susan B. Turkel. "Integrating Arithmetic and Geometry with Numbered Points on a Circle." *Arithmetic Teacher* 36 (January 1989): 28–30.

Geometric figures are formed when twelve equally spaced points on a circle are numbered consecutively and joined according to some pattern. Employs polygons, factors, patterns, and prediction.

O'Daffer, Phares G., and Randall I. Charles. "Problem Solving: Tips for Teachers: Asking Questions to Evaluate Problem Solving." *Arithmetic Teacher* 35 (January 1988): 26–27.

Outlines types of questions to ask to help evaluate various stages of problem solving. Includes several examples and a checklist.

Peck, Donald M., Stanley M. Jencks, and Michael L. Connell. "Improving Instruction through Brief Interviews." *Arithmetic Teacher* 37 (November 1989): 15–17.

Describes the use of brief interviews to determine which children in a fifth-grade classroom had acquired the concept of division, which applied a mechanical process, and which showed evidence of both.

Richardson, Kathy. "Assessing Understanding." *Arithmetic Teacher* 35 (February 1988): 39–41.

Discusses the importance of questioning children to determine if their performance on computational tasks is based on understanding or rote learning.

Sanfiorenzo, Norberto R. (March 1991). See entry under ***"Patterns, Relations, Functions, and Algebra."***

Schultz, James E. "Area Models—Spanning the Mathematics of Grades 3–9." *Arithmetic Teacher* 39 (October 1991): 42–46.

Discusses the use of the area model for multiplication, distributive property, prime numbers, fractions, and probability.

Silverman, Helene. "Ideas." *Arithmetic Teacher* 37 (September 1989): 26–32.

Names of real and fictional people are used to develop simple graphs, explore symmetry, and count.

———. "Ideas." *Arithmetic Teacher* 37 (November 1989): 26–32.

Flags form the basis for exploring area and perimeter, reading maps, and solving problems.

———. "Ideas." *Arithmetic Teacher* 37 (January 1990): 19–24.

Activities involve map reading, geography, language, and coordinate graphing.

———. "Ideas." *Arithmetic Teacher* 37 (May 1990): 18–24.

Constellations are used to explore polygons and angles.

Spence, Carolyn, and Carol S. Martin. "Mathematics + Social Studies = Learning Connections." *Arithmetic Teacher* 36 (December 1988): 2–5.

Children explore urban geography, measurement, graphing, and architecture while building a model town.

Sullivan, Peter, and David Clarke. "Catering to All Abilities through 'Good' Questions." *Arithmetic Teacher* 39 (October 1991): 14–18.

Presents examples of nonalgorithmic problems that lend themselves to mixed-ability classes. Students' responses and management suggestions are included.

Szetela, Walter. "The Problem of Evaluation in Problem Solving: Can We Find Solutions?" *Arithmetic Teacher* 35 (November 1987): 36–41.

Compares various models for evaluating problem solving. Suggestions for developing one's own scheme are given.

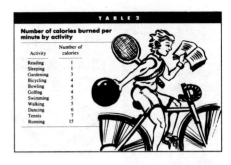

Moniuszko, 1991

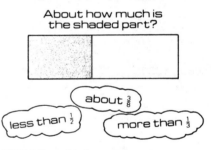

NCTM *Standards*, p. 58

Spence and Martin, 1988

NCTM *Standards*, p. 60

Wilde, 1991

	Order of symmetry	
Internal design	Line	Rotational
A–1 flower	7	7
A–2 pinwheel	0	10
A–3 leaf	1	1
A–4 center flower	16	8
A–5 sprig	0	1

TABLE 2

Zaslavsky, 1990

Taylor, Lyn, Ellen Stevens, John J. Peregoy, and Barbara Bath. "American Indians, Mathematical Attitudes, and the *Standards*." *Arithmetic Teacher* 38 (February 1991): 14–21.

Instructions are given for designs, tessellations, and number patterns derived from Native American culture.

Thiessen, Diane. "Problem Solving: Tips for Teachers: Value Lies in Writing Word Problems." *Arithmetic Teacher* 35 (November 1987): 34–35.

Offers suggestions for writing problems from diagrams and ways to identify "key words that aren't." Lists five other articles on the topic.

Tischler, Rosamond Welchman. "Mathematics from Children's Literature." *Arithmetic Teacher* 35 (February 1988): 42–47.

Describes the use of children's literature to motivate young students in mathematical tasks. Activities employ acting skills, manipulatives, guess-the-rule games, one-to-one matching, counting, and hypothesizing. The simple materials are easy to obtain.

Van de Walle, John A. "Problem Solving: Tips for Teachers: Hands-On Thinking Activities for Young Children." *Arithmetic Teacher* 35 (February 1988): 62–63.

Recommends a variety of geometry and measurement problems for young children. Attribute blocks, geoboards, and other materials are used.

Wilde, Sandra. "Learning to Write about Mathematics." *Arithmetic Teacher* 38 (February 1991): 38–43.

Explores the value of writing to help clarify concepts and furnish diagnostic information; some examples are from a bilingual classroom.

Woodward, Ernest, Sandra Frost, and Anita Smith. "Cemetery Mathematics." *Arithmetic Teacher* 39 (December 1991): 31–36.

Describes how students in grades 4, 5, and 6 collected data from tombstones in a local cemetery and used the data to develop and interpret graphs and explore simple probability.

Young, Sharon L. "Ideas." *Arithmetic Teacher* 38 (September 1990): 23–33.

Uses data about dinosaurs to explore measurement and graphs.

_____. "Ideas." *Arithmetic Teacher* 38 (November 1990): 23–32.

Integrates sports, science, mathematics, statistics, graphs, and language.

_____. "Ideas." *Arithmetic Teacher* 38 (December 1990): 23–33.

Bicycles are the subject of measurement and data collection and analysis; they are used to introduce mathematics vocabulary.

_____. "Ideas." *Arithmetic Teacher* 38 (March 1991): 24–33.

Fingerprint patterns are analyzed for identifiable patterns and frequency.

_____. "Ideas." *Arithmetic Teacher* 38 (May 1991): 25–33.

Data on television viewing are collected, organized, graphed, and interpreted.

Zaslavsky, Claudia. "People Who Live in Round Houses." *Arithmetic Teacher* 37 (September 1989): 18–21.

Explores shapes of different houses around the world. Children investigate advantages and disadvantages of each. Incorporates visual arts and social studies.

_____. "Symmetry in American Folk Art." *Arithmetic Teacher* 38 (September 1990): 6–12.

The American quilt is the basis for a study of pattern, symmetry, and transformations.

_____. "Multicultural Mathematics Education for the Middle Grades." *Arithmetic Teacher* 38 (February 1991): 8–13.

Projects in measurement and graph theory are adapted from aspects of Third World cultures.

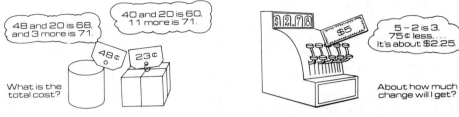

Zepp, Raymond A. "Real-Life Business Math at Enterprise Village." *Arithmetic Teacher* 39 (December 1991): 10–14.

Describes a simulated economic community developed by a school board. Students are offered various "employment" opportunities and experiences with various aspects of economic realities.

NCTM *Standards*, p. 45   **NCTM** *Standards*, p. 45

Number (number sense, operations, estimation, fractions, and decimals)

Akaishi, Amy, and Mark Saul. "Exploring, Learning, Sharing: Vignettes from the Classroom." *Arithmetic Teacher* 39 (November 1991): 12–16.

Second graders are introduced to fractions while deciding how to share apple pies. Other real-life situations are used to explore other concepts, including tallying and division.

Arithmetic Teacher 36 (February 1989). Focus issue on number sense.

Articles define teaching, promoting, and applying number sense. Discusses the importance of number sense for estimation, problem solving, measurement, calculator use, and an understanding of place value.

Bobis, Janette F. "Using a Calculator to Develop Number Sense." *Arithmetic Teacher* 38 (January 1991): 42–45.

Describes estimation and mental-mathematics procedures to help students judge the reasonableness of answers.

Chick, Andrea. "Readers' Dialogue: Schoolwide Estimations." *Arithmetic Teacher* 38 (November 1990): 2.

Second graders estimate the number of students needed to form a chain around the school.

Cramer, Kathleen, and Nadine Bezuk. "Multiplication of Fractions: Teaching for Understanding." *Arithmetic Teacher* 39 (November 1991): 34–37.

This analysis of the procedures involved in multiplication explores ways of using various models of real-life situations to lead to the use of written and spoken symbols.

Esty, Warren W. "One Point of View: The Least Common Denominator." *Arithmetic Teacher* 39 (December 1991): 6–7.

Suggests that a stress on teaching the lowest common denominator is detrimental to students' understanding of addition and subtraction of fractions. Proposes an alternative technique that is more easily generalizable.

Goldenberg, E. Paul. "A Mathematical Conversation with Fourth Graders." *Arithmetic Teacher* 38 (April 1991): 38–43.

Describes how children developed concepts of decimals through problem solving with calculators. Problems explore density of numbers, comparing and ordering of decimals, and the use of successive-approximation techniques.

Goldman, Phyllis H. "Teaching Arithmetic Averaging: An Activity Approach." *Arithmetic Teacher* 37 (March 1990): 38–43.

Children share cardboard "cookies" and write about their findings while exploring averaging through cooperative problem-solving activities.

Gluck, Doris H. "Helping Students Understand Place Value." *Arithmetic Teacher* 38 (March 1991): 10–13.

Describes how to use successively more abstract concrete materials to lead children from simple counting to an understanding of place value and correct use of necessary symbols.

FIGURE 3

Taking a "magnifying glass" to the space between 6.5 and 6.6, we see some more numbers.

6	36	6.5
6.1	37.21	6.51
6.2		6.52
6.3		6.53
6.4		6.54
6.5		6.55
6.6		6.56
6.7		6.57
6.8		6.58
6.9	47.61	6.59
7	49	6.6

Goldenberg, 1991

Anton, Juanita, and Booker want to share 6 cookies equally. How many cookies does each one get?

NCTM *Standards*, p. 41

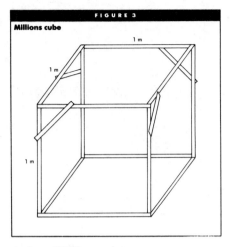

FIGURE 3
Millions cube

1 m
1 m
1 m

Joslyn, 1990

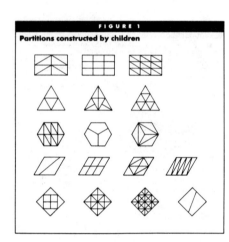

FIGURE 1
Partitions constructed by children

Pothier and Sawada, 1990

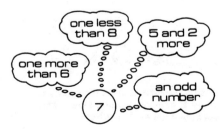

NCTM *Standards*, p. 39

Irons, Calvin, and Rosemary Irons. "Ideas." *Arithmetic Teacher* 39 (December 1991): 18–25.

Activities explore uses of numbers, sizes of numbers, and types of numbers in a post office, in an airport, or in sports.

Joslyn, Ruth E. "Using Concrete Models to Teach Large-Number Concepts." *Arithmetic Teacher* 38 (November 1990): 6–9.

Describes an extension of base-ten blocks to help fourth and fifth graders visualize large numbers. A cubic meter is used as the model for one million.

Kamii, Constance, and Barbara A. Lewis. "Research into Practice: Constructivism and First-Grade Arithmetic." *Arithmetic Teacher* 38 (September 1990): 36–37.

Asserts that children should be encouraged to develop their own ways of interpreting numbers and that paper-pencil computation interferes with such development.

Lindquist, Mary Montgomery. "Estimation and Mental Computation: Measurement." *Arithmetic Teacher* 34 (January 1987): 16–17.

Strategies for estimation are presented. Teaching tips and classroom examples are included.

Nibbelink, William H. "Teaching Equations." *Arithmetic Teacher* 38 (November 1990): 48–51.

Suggests that one reason for children's difficulty with equations is the horizontal format. Outlines a progression in vocabulary and concept development to help students acquire greater competence.

Ott, Jack M. "A Unified Approach to Multiplying Fractions." *Arithmetic Teacher* 37 (March 1990): 47–49.

Argues that different interpretations of multiplication as applied to fractions and whole numbers could be at the core of students' difficulties with multiplication of fractions.

Ott, Jack M., Daniel L. Snook, and Diana L. Gibson. "Understanding Partitive Division of Fractions." *Arithmetic Teacher* 39 (October 1991): 7–11.

Explores concrete experiences that help children in developing an understanding of division with fractions.

Parker, Janet, and Connie Carroll Widmer. "Teaching Mathematics with Technology: How Big Is a Million?" *Arithmetic Teacher* 39 (September 1991): 38–41.

Uses concrete materials, calculators, and spreadsheets to help students acquire a better concept of large numbers.

Pothier, Yvonne, and Daiyo Sawada. "Partitioning: An Approach to Fractions." *Arithmetic Teacher* 38 (December 1990): 12–16.

Children use paper folding, drawing, and dissection to explore concepts of fractions, geometric figures, motion geometry, and figurate numbers.

Rees, Jocelyn Marie. "Two-Sided Pies: Help for Improper Fractions and Mixed Numbers." *Arithmetic Teacher* 35 (December 1987): 28–32.

Describes a model children can use to display mixed numbers and improper fractions and show their equivalences; the model can also be used for comparing and ordering mixed numbers.

Rubenstein, Rheta. "Estimation and Mental Computation: Compatible Numbers." *Arithmetic Teacher* 34 (May 1987): 24–25.

Compares the use of compatible numbers with rounding and front-end estimation. Stresses value of several possible answers.

Schoen, Harold L. "Estimation and Mental Computation: Front-End Estimation." *Arithmetic Teacher* 34 (February 1987): 28–29.

Describes the steps in front-end estimation: identify highest place value, mentally compute, and adjust the estimate.

Singer, Rita. "Estimation and Counting in the Block Corner." *Arithmetic Teacher* 35 (January 1988): 10–14.

Children estimate how many sets of five blocks they must put away at clean-up time. Includes tallying, predicting, and counting.

Sowder, Judith T. "Mental Computation and Number Sense." *Arithmetic Teacher* 37 (March 1990): 18–20.

Endorses the introduction of mental computation at an early age as a valuable precursor to the development of number sense and formal algorithms. Invented mental procedures are considered a reflection of a child's thinking.

Steffe, Leslie P., and John Olive. "Research into Practice: The Problem of Fractions in the Elementary School." *Arithmetic Teacher* 38 (May 1991): 22–24.

Describes ways in which children construct "prefractional" concepts and how those concepts can affect their understanding of fractions.

Sutton, John T., and Tonya D. Urbatsch. "Transition Boards: A Good Idea Made Better." *Arithmetic Teacher* 38 (January 1991): 4–8.

Proposes a work mat for use with base-ten blocks that encourages children to see the inverse natures of addition and subtraction.

Thompson, Frances. "Two-Digit Addition and Subtraction: What Works?" *Arithmetic Teacher* 38 (January 1991): 10–13.

Compares results of exposing second graders to various methods of two-digit subtraction with regrouping. Concludes that extended work with manipulatives is necessary and links with the abstract should be carefully modeled.

Trafton, Paul R., and Judy Zawojewski. "Estimation and Mental Computation: Rounding Wisely." *Arithmetic Teacher* 34 (April 1987): 36–37.

Emphasizes the need for flexible thinking when using rounding.

Van de Walle, John A. "The Early Development of Number Relations." *Arithmetic Teacher* 35 (February 1988): 15–21, 32.

Describes ways of helping children develop number concepts through use of patterned sets, "number machines," dot cards, and other materials.

Van Erp, Jos W. M. "The Power of Five: An Alternative Model." *Arithmetic Teacher* 38 (April 1991): 48–53.

Discusses the importance of mental imagery in developing computation skills. Describes a successful technique of moving from manipulatives to physical action to mental action.

Space and Dimension (geometry, spatial sense, and measurement)

Arithmetic Teacher 37 (February 1990). Focus issue on spatial sense.

Articles define spatial sense and suggest several ideas to help children develop spatial abilities and communicate about them. Includes activities with tangrams, geoboards, and blocks.

Barnett, Carne S. (January 1991). See entry under **"Themes That Cut across Mathematics."**

Battista, Michael T., and Douglas H. Clements. "Research into Practice: Constructing Geometric Concepts in Logo." *Arithmetic Teacher* 38 (November 1990): 15–17.

Uses technology to develop concepts of turns and angles. Gives students' verbal descriptions of turtle's movements.

_____. "Research into Practice: Using Spatial Imagery in Geometric Reasoning." *Arithmetic Teacher* 39 (November 1991): 18–21.

Describes how students use spatial visualization to determine which of a collection of figures can be drawn using simple Logo procedures. Children test their predictions and explain the results.

Binswanger, Richard. "Discovering Perimeter and Area with Logo." *Arithmetic Teacher* 36 (September 1988): 18–24.

Discovery activities relate fixed perimeters to varying areas and vice versa.

Bright, George W. "Teaching Mathematics with Technology: Logo and Geometry." *Arithmetic Teacher* 36 (January 1989): 32–34.

Logo is used to explore angles, positions, and shapes.

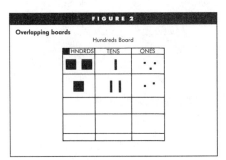

Sutton and Urbatsch, 1991

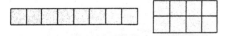

Only one rectangle can be made with seven tiles, so 7 is prime.

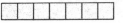

More than one rectangle can be made with eight tiles, so 8 is composite.

NCTM *Standards*, p. 93

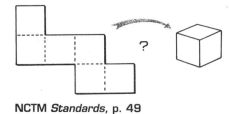

NCTM *Standards*, p. 49

NCTM *Standards,* p. 49

FIGURE 1

A tessellation

Giganti and Cittadino, 1990

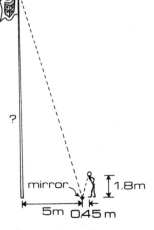

mirror   1.8m

5m   0.45 m

Indirect measurement

NCTM *Standards,* p. 119

Burger, William F. "One Point of View: An Active Approach to Geometry." *Arithmetic Teacher* 36 (November 1988): 2.

Advocates a concrete approach to geometry in elementary grades and a greater recognition of the importance of geometric concepts in both mathematics and real life.

Carroll, William M. "Cross Sections of Clay Solids." *Arithmetic Teacher* 35 (March 1988): 6–11.

Furnishes ideas for predicting and verifying shapes of cross sections of various geometric solids.

Chancellor, Dinah. "Calendar Mathematics: Time and Time Again." *Arithmetic Teacher* 39 (January 1992):14–15.

Problems for levels K–2, 3–5, and 6–8 explore various aspects of time and telling time. Topics include time zones, sundials, and the length of a minute.

Clauss, Judith Enz. "Pentagonal Tessellations." *Arithmetic Teacher* 38 (January 1991): 52–56.

Examines pentagons that tessellate, those that don't, and reasons for differences. Discusses angles, transformations, and symmetry.

Cook, Marcy. "Ideas." *Arithmetic Teacher* 36 (April 1989): 27–32.

Real-world applications are based on weight and temperature data. Activities involve graphing, patterns, and relationships.

Fay, Nancy, and Catherine Tsairides. "Metric Mall." *Arithmetic Teacher* 37 (September 1989): 6–11.

This integrated mathematics-science unit includes topics of linear measurement, area, mass, volume, and capacity. Cooperative learning groups are used.

Giganti, Paul, Jr., and Mary Jo Cittadino. "The Art of Tessellation." *Arithmetic Teacher* 37 (March 1990): 6–16.

This comprehensive introduction to tessellation activities includes sample worksheets and extensive references.

Jamski, William D. "Six Hard Pieces." *Arithmetic Teacher* 37 (October 1989): 34–35.

Employs tangram pieces to explore area relations by constructing squares of different sizes.

Juraschek, William. "Get in Touch with Shape." *Arithmetic Teacher* 37 (April 1990): 14–16.

Cubes are manipulated to develop spatial sense through tactile and visual exploration and construction of two-dimensional drawings.

Kaiser, Barbara. "Explorations with Tessellating Polygons." *Arithmetic Teacher* 36 (December 1988): 19–24.

Describes explorations in transformations, angle measurement, and relationships through tessellations.

Kriegler, Shelley. "The Tangram—It's More Than an Ancient Puzzle." *Arithmetic Teacher* 38 (May 1991): 38–43.

Uses tangrams to explore coordinate graphing and scale drawing through cooperative-group activities.

Langbort, Carol R. "Jar Lids—an Unusual Math Manipulative." *Arithmetic Teacher* 36 (November 1988): 22–25.

Activities use jar lids for sorting, classifying, graphing, and measuring diameters and circumferences.

Lappan, Glenda, and Ruhama Even. "Research into Practice: Similarity in the Middle Grades." *Arithmetic Teacher* 35 (May 1988): 32–35.

Discusses the importance of similarity, difficulties students have with the concept, and activities that use concrete materials to develop the concept.

Larke, Patricia J. "Geometric Extravaganza: Spicing Up Geometry." *Arithmetic Teacher* 36 (September 1988): 12–16.

Describes the phases of planning and conducting a geometry fair.

Lindquist, Mary Montgomery (January 1987). See entry under **"Number."**

Neufeld, K. Allen. "Body Measurement." *Arithmetic Teacher* 36 (May 1989): 12–15.

Using measures of their own bodies, students investigate surface area, volume, mass, and density.

Nevin, Mary Lou. "Ideas." *Arithmetic Teacher* 39 (January 1992):16–22, 27–32.

Students use regular and nonregular polygons to create symmetric patterns and tessellations. Classifying of angles and triangles emerges in a natural way.

Onslow, Barry. "Pentominoes Revisited." *Arithmetic Teacher* 37 (May 1990): 5–9.

Describes several activities to use with pentominoes, including symmetry explorations and tessellations.

Prentice, Gerard. "Flexible Straws." *Arithmetic Teacher* 37 (November 1989): 4–5.

Students use flexible straws to construct two- and three-dimensional figures.

Taylor, Lyn, et al. (February 1991). See entry under **"Themes That Cut across Mathematics."**

Wheatley, Grayson H. "Research into Practice: Enhancing Mathematics Learning through Imagery." *Arithmetic Teacher* 39 (September 1991): 34–36.

Describes how imagery can be applied in all areas of mathematics. Discusses how students' implicit images can lead them astray. Suggests activities to help students develop and use imagery.

Wilson, Patricia S., and Verna M. Adams. "A Dynamic Way to Teach Angle and Angle Measure." *Arithmetic Teacher* 39 (January 1992): 6–13.

Students use flexible straws and other manipulatives to explore angles in the classroom, compare angles, and eventually develop a method for measuring them. "Protractors" are created by using congruent sectors of a circle.

Young, Sharon L. (September 1990, November 1990, December 1990). See entries under **"Themes That Cut across Mathematics."**

Zaslavsky, Claudia (September 1989, September 1990, February 1991). See entries under **"Themes That Cut across Mathematics."**

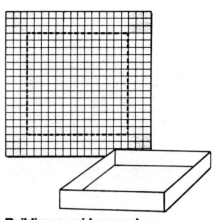

Building a grid-paper box
NCTM *Standards*, p. 80

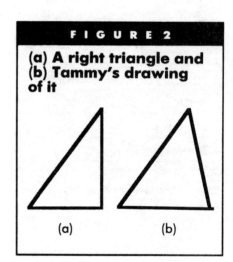

FIGURE 2
(a) A right triangle and (b) Tammy's drawing of it

(a)　　　(b)

Wheatley, 1991

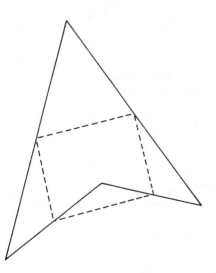
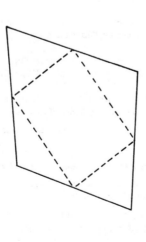
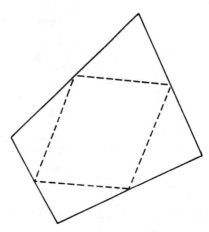

NCTM *Standards*, p. 114

BASIC

```
10 NF = 6
20 X = INT(RND(4) * NF) + 1
30 Y = INT(RND(4) * NF) + 1
40 SUM = X + Y
50 PRINT X, Y, SUM
60 END
```

Logo

```
TO ROLL.DICE
   MAKE "NF 6
   MAKE "X 1 + RANDOM :NF
   MAKE "Y 1 + RANDOM :NF
   MAKE "SUM :X + :Y
   PRINT SE SE :X :Y :SUM
END
```

Bright, 1989

Survey	
Harry	Vanilla
Molly	Chocolate
Ted	Chocolate
José	Strawberry

Flavor Choices					
Vanilla	X	X	X		
Chocolate	X	X	X	X	X
Strawberry	X	X			

What is the favorite flavor of ice cream in our class?

NCTM *Standards*, p. 55

Time	0	10	20	30	40	5
People told	2	4	8	16	32	
Total	2	6	14	30		

NCTM *Standards*, p. 99

Data Collection and Interpretation (statistics and probability)

Barnett, Carne S. (January 1991). See entry under ***"Themes That Cut across Mathematics."***

Borasi, Raffaella. "Olympic Medal Counts: A Glimpse into Humanistic Aspects of Mathematics." *Arithmetic Teacher* 37 (November 1989): 47–52.

Discusses affective issues related to mathematics and describes a real-life activity involving interpreting and reporting data.

Bright, George W. "Teaching Mathematics with Technology: Probability Simulations." *Arithmetic Teacher* 36 (May 1989): 16–18.

A short program in BASIC or Logo is used to generate data for probability activities with students.

Chancellor, Dinah. "Calendar Mathematics: Taking Chances." *Arithmetic Teacher* 39 (November 1991): 22–23.

Suggests activities for students to do in groups to explore some fundamental ideas in probability.

Cook, Marcy (April 1989). See entry under ***"Space and Dimension."***

Irons, Calvin, and Rosemary Irons. "Ideas." *Arithmetic Teacher* 39 (October 1991): 26–33.

Activities involve interpreting several types of graphs. Questions involve higher-level thinking as well as basic reading of data.

Pagni, David L. "A Television Programming Challenge: A Cooperative Group Activity That Uses Mathematics." *Arithmetic Teacher* 36 (January 1989): 7–9.

In this interdisciplinary activity students gather and analyze data related to television viewing, then make suggestions on the basis of their analysis.

Schielack, Jane F. "Teaching Mathematics with Technology: A Graphing Tool for the Primary Grades." *Arithmetic Teacher* 38 (October 1990): 40–43.

Young students generate computer graphs of real-life data. Manipulatives are used along with computers.

Schultz, James E. (October 1991). See entry under ***"Themes That Cut across Mathematics."***

Shulte, Albert P. "Research Report: Learning Probability Concepts in Elementary School Mathematics." *Arithmetic Teacher* 34 (January 1987): 32–33.

Reviews the research to identify what students can learn about probability with instruction and what they may have learned without instruction.

Silverman, Helene. "Ideas." *Arithmetic Teacher* 37 (December 1989): 27–32.

Students obtain information from maps and interpret and record data on charts.

_____. "Ideas." *Arithmetic Teacher* 37 (April 1990): 27–32.

Games generate data for analysis. Students tally, graph, and find the median and range.

Woodward, Ernest, Sandra Frost, and Anita Smith (December 1991). See entry under ***"Themes That Cut across Mathematics."***

Young, Sharon L. (September 1990, November 1990, December 1990, March 1991, May 1991). See entries under ***"Themes That Cut across Mathematics."***

Zawojewski, Judith S. "Research into Practice: Teaching Statistics: Mean, Median, and Mode." *Arithmetic Teacher* 35 (March 1988): 25–26.

Real-life applications of mean, median, and mode are based on research findings.

Patterns, Relations, Functions, and Algebra

Bright, George W. "Teaching Mathematics with Technology: Exploring Patterns." *Arithmetic Teacher* 36 (November 1988): 56–57.

Describes procedures to generate graphs and numerical patterns with Logo and BASIC. Patterns are extended with calculators.

Cook, Marcy. "Ideas." *Arithmetic Teacher* 36 (October 1988): 31–36.

Given two examples, students use exactly ten tiles (with digits 0–9) to discover and extend a rule.

Duncan, David R., and Bonnie H. Litwiller. "Number-Lattice Polygons and Patterns: Sums and Products." *Arithmetic Teacher* 37 (January 1990): 14–15.

Gives instructions for discovering patterns by comparing sums of interior numbers and sums of numbers on the perimeter of a hexagon drawn on a number grid.

Feinberg, Miriam M. "Using Patterns to Practice Basic Facts." *Arithmetic Teacher* 37 (April 1990): 38–41.

Patterns on the hundred chart, number sequences, and unusual properties of 9 are among the ideas explored.

Kieran, Carolyn. "Research into Practice: Helping to Make the Transition to Algebra." *Arithmetic Teacher* 38 (March 1991): 49–51.

Asserts the importance of students' thoroughly understanding arithmetic before they attempt to generalize to algebraic statements.

Litwiller, Bonnie H., and David R. Duncan. "Rhombus Ratio Activities." *Arithmetic Teacher* 38 (March 1991): 39–41.

Patterns in addition and multiplication grids are used to generate equivalent ratios.

Loewen, A. C. "Lima Beans, Paper Cups, and Algebra." *Arithmetic Teacher* 38 (April 1991): 34–37.

Describes the use of simple manipulatives to develop the meaning of variables and of equations. Two colors of beans are used to illustrate opposites and include negative values in equations.

Nibbelink, William H. (November 1990). See entry under **"Number."**

Norman, F. Alexander. "Figurate Numbers in the Classroom." *Arithmetic Teacher* 38 (March 1991): 42–45.

Triangular, square, and hexagonal numbers are explored on dot papers and with the computer. Students predict and check results.

Pagni, David L. "Teaching Mathematics with Technology: Teaching Mathematics Using Calculators." *Arithmetic Teacher* 38 (January 1991): 58–60.

Explores mathematical relationships through the use of "constant" keys on calculators and the resulting patterns.

Sanfiorenzo, Norberto R. "Evaluating Expressions: A Problem-solving Approach." *Arithmetic Teacher* 38 (March 1991): 34–35.

Describes computation problems designed to illustrate the importance of brackets as grouping symbols.

Taylor, Lyn, et al. (February 1991). See entry under **"Themes That Cut across Mathematics."**

Feinberg, 1990

Loewen, 1991

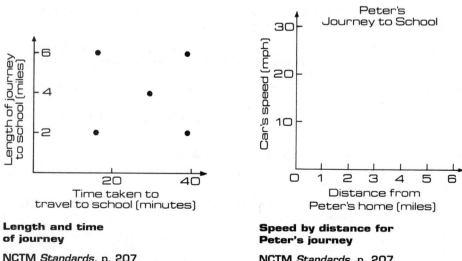

Length and time of journey

NCTM *Standards*, p. 207

Speed by distance for Peter's journey

NCTM *Standards*, p. 207